Saints and Holy Places of Yorkshire

A Pilgrims' Guide to God's Own County

— GAVIN WAKEFIELD —

Sacristy
Press

Sacristy Press
PO Box 612, Durham, DH1 9HT

www.sacristy.co.uk

First published in 2020 by Sacristy Press, Durham

Sacristy Limited, registered in England & Wales, number 7565667

British Library Cataloguing-in-Publication Data
A catalogue record for the book is available from the British Library

ISBN 978-1-78959-103-3

To Fran, who has journeyed throughout Yorkshire with me and helped me to love the places and the people.

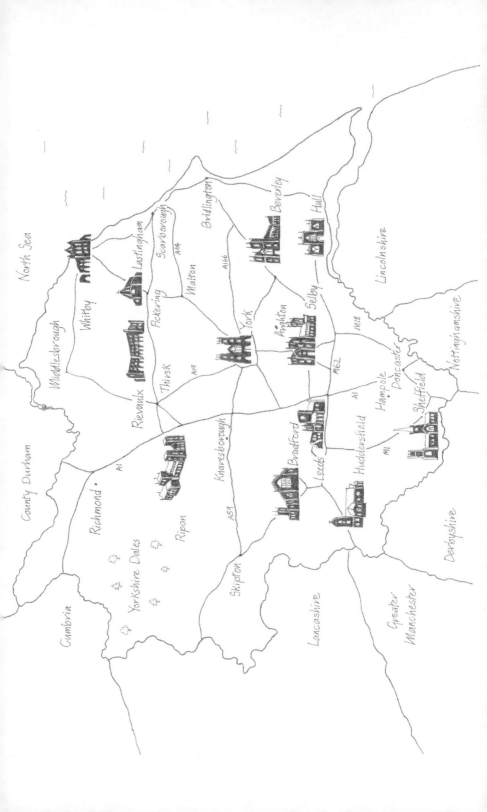

Contents

Acknowledgements

Over a long period of time many people have helped me to learn more about Yorkshire, its saints and holy places. I want to thank them for sharing with me their insight and encouragement. Among them are Angela Bailey, David Casswell, Geraldine Casswell, Lynn Comer, Catherine Copp, John Dobson, Jeremy Fletcher, Robin Gamble, Lynn Hellmuth, David Hogan, John Thomson, Ann Walton, Richard Walton, John Weetman.

I am especially grateful to those who have read and offered feedback on substantial portions of the text: Andrew de Smet, Rachel Eden, John Pritchard, Fran Wakefield, Sarah Wakefield, and finally Alan Bartlett, who read through it all and told me what he thought of it! The map of Yorkshire was drawn by Geraldine Casswell in response to her reading of the manuscript—many thanks. Finally, thanks to Natalie Watson and the staff at Sacristy Press for their help and encouragement.

The sections on Hilda, Cedd and Wilfrid are developed from material in an earlier book of mine, *Holy Places, Holy People* (Oxford: Lion Hudson, 2008).

Any errors of fact or judgement that remain are down to me.

Introduction: The people and the places

I am not a true Yorkshireman—there, I've admitted it. I wasn't born in God's Own County. But I have lived at different times in South Yorkshire, East Yorkshire and York for much of my adult life, and I have family connections in West Yorkshire and North Yorkshire, all of which have given me a love for the people and places of the county. I value the sense of pride so many Yorkshire people have for the places they live in and care for, and in this book I hope to add another layer of appreciation. As you would expect, there is a lot of reflective material here, but I am also going to claim that this is (probably) the first book of Christian pilgrimage to include a chocolate trail!

Much of today's Yorkshire character and landscape has significant roots in its Christian heritage. The romantic ruins of abbeys on the cliffs at Whitby, the steep valleys at Fountains and Rievaulx and the great cathedrals and churches of Ripon, Beverley and York exist only because God's Own People (in all their complexity and quirkiness) have made them possible. So I want to celebrate and remember some of those people, to retell their stories and connect them with places, some of which are obvious and some surprising.

I have tried to select a range of people from over the centuries who have made significant contributions to the life of Yorkshire and often beyond. In many cases, these are characters whose stories have long inspired or challenged me, while a few are relatively new to me and have been a delight to add to my own appreciation of Yorkshire's history.

When describing this book to friends I've used the shorthand of saying "It's a book of Yorkshire saints, but not necessarily saints in the way we always understand the word." All the people in this book understood themselves to be Christians, and some of them have been officially designated as saints. However, God's Own People are more than priests, nuns and monks: you will also meet a king and a housewife, a lawyer and a plumber, a few business entrepreneurs and a politician. They represent many other people who have helped to form the Yorkshire character and landscape in ways that reflect their Christian commitment as they understood it in their own time. As I tell their stories I have tried to include a few thoughts on how their lives have something to say to mine and, I hope, to yours too.

How you might use the book

This book is a sequel to my earlier *Holy Places, Holy People* (Lion Hudson, 2008) which tells the stories of people and places in the North East of England. Like that book it is set out in the form of a seven-day pilgrimage, and in the next section I suggest how this might be possible using a car. In reality, I know that most people have used *Holy Places, Holy People* as a guide for day visits and as short inspirational pieces on each character, perhaps read on a daily basis.

Each chapter has a similar structure. There are four main elements: the stories of the People, Places associated with the People in this book, a short Prayer which picks up some of the themes, and some Practicalities for making a visit. Because there are so many interesting sites, I have included bonus material at the end of each chapter about other places you might want to visit. In some cases, I have been able to mention pilgrimage routes, and it is worth checking websites as these are continuing to develop. As I write this, 2020 has been designated a year of pilgrimage by many cathedrals, and there is a significant interest in walking to these places. The British Pilgrimage Trust promotes pilgrimage to holy places and provides details of many routes, not just to Christian sites (see <https://britishpilgrimage.org>).

A possible itinerary for a week-long pilgrimage (by car!)

For many readers this book may be enjoyed as a pilgrimage in the imagination, and others who live locally may want to use it for day trips. However, with a bit of planning it is possible to travel through God's Own County in the week suggested and to visit at least one site connected with the main characters. The journey is mostly possible by bus and train, but may not quite fit into a week, as some of the places do not have regular or even any public transport.

This is only a suggestion, and it does not include the additional places mentioned at the end of each day. Before trying it out, please read the book as a whole and consider any travel and accommodation arrangements you wish to have. Some details of the locations are included at the end of each chapter.

Travel to Whitby and stay overnight

Day 1
Morning: Whitby Abbey and St Mary's Church
Lunch: on the way to or at Lastingham
Afternoon: Lastingham and Rievaulx Abbey
Overnight: Helmsley, or somewhere on the way to Beverley, such as
    Malton

Day 2
Morning: Beverley Minster and St Mary's Church
Lunch: Beverley
Afternoon: Hull Minster and Wilberforce House
Overnight: Hull

Day 3

Morning: Aughton. Travel into York

Lunch: York

Afternoon: York Minster and St Michael-le-Belfrey

Overnight: York

Day 4

Explore York

Suggestions: The Bar Convent Museum and chapel, the shrine of
    Margaret Clitherow in the Shambles, and Friargate Meeting House
    (Quaker) for the link with Joseph Rowntree

Overnight: travel on to the vicinity of Knaresborough

Day 5

Morning: Robert Flower's Cave, Knaresborough. Ripon Cathedral

Lunch: Ripon

Afternoon: Fountains Abbey

Overnight: I suggest travelling south in preparation for the next day.
    This is the most awkward transition of the week, because we reach
    the built-up area along the M62 corridor

Day 6

Morning: Huddersfield Parish Church

Lunch: Bradford

Afternoon: home of Smith Wigglesworth and Lister Park; possibly the
    statue of Richard Oastler and Bradford Cathedral in the city centre

Overnight: travel on to the vicinity of Selby, preferably avoiding the
    busiest period on the M62!

Day 7

Morning: Selby Abbey

Lunch: visit Hampole and have lunch in Adwick-le-Street

Afternoon: Sheffield Cathedral and the end of the pilgrimage.

Christianity in Yorkshire:
A very short history

The purpose of this section is to offer an overview of the history of Christianity in Yorkshire, so that the individual stories can be fitted into a bigger picture. It is not trying to cover everything or everyone but to give a framework for the rest of the book. The timeline that follows may also help in following the storyline.

Christianity probably spread to Roman Britain initially through traders and soldiers in the first Christian century, and it is very likely that small Christian communities formed in Yorkshire at an early stage. The first direct evidence of a Christian group in the region is the mention of a bishop of York attending a church council in France in 314. Presumably at least a few churches existed for the next century under the Roman Empire, and it is likely that they continued for longer than that. However, Christianity was pushed westward and northward when the pagan Angles invaded, and we know almost nothing of Christianity in Yorkshire until the seventh century.

As the Saxon and Anglian kingdoms developed, they began to turn towards Christianity, partly through political pressure and the desire to form marriage alliances. In 625 King Edwin married a Christian princess from Kent and received a bishop, Paulinus, as part of the deal. This led to the adoption of the Christian faith by leading families and the building of the first church on the site of the present York Minster. It was not all straightforward: warfare caused Bishop Paulinus to flee with surviving members of the royal family, and another strand of Christianity arrived from Ireland, via Scotland. Missionaries like Aidan and his followers spread their understanding of the faith across what is now the north of England and southern Scotland. Disagreements over certain aspects of faith, like the dating of Easter, were resolved at the Synod of Whitby in 664 in favour of Roman observance. The wise guidance of Hilda and Cuthbert enabled a creative synthesis to develop, and Christianity became more firmly established. Viking raids, first on Lindisfarne in 793, and then in more widespread areas, led to the destruction of many monasteries and their libraries. However, by this stage the Church was strong enough to survive the attacks, and by the tenth century many Vikings had become Christians themselves.

The Norman invasion of England in 1066 was a major turning point in the history of the country. Yorkshire was one of the places that resisted Norman rule, and William the Conqueror felt it necessary to enact a scorched-earth policy, known as the "Harrying of the North", in order to crush the resistance. Villages were burnt down, people forced off their land or slaughtered, and fields salted so they would be unproductive for years to come. In some places, recovery was very slow, though in others the new Norman overlords invested heavily in castles, churches and monasteries. Even now the churches and monasteries in the countryside and the big urban churches are mainly those built between about 1100 and 1500. Yorkshire became a particular centre for monastic life, both in the towns and in the countryside, and on this pilgrimage we will visit a number of the more dramatic sites such as Whitby, Rievaulx and Fountains. During this period church life was aligned much more closely with that of Western Europe and its practices affected every part of daily life.

At the time of the Reformation in the sixteenth century there was something of a split between the north and the south of England: the dissolution of the monasteries in the 1530s under Henry VIII was especially brutal in Yorkshire, because so much of the local economy and the welfare of ordinary people were dependent on them. There was also a stronger attachment to the familiar rituals of the Roman Catholic Church, and this led to repeated uprisings. The most serious was called the Pilgrimage of Grace, and it came close to overthrowing Henry's rule. We will learn something of it in the story of Robert Aske.

Even though Henry VIII survived that rebellion, commitment to the old religion continued in York and in the countryside. Some became martyrs for their faith, others lived this out more quietly and secretly. Though he does not feature as a saint in this book it is telling that Guy

Fawkes, one of the key Catholic plotters against James I, was brought up in York and nurtured in the Catholic faith. Over time greater tolerance for Nonconformists on the one hand and Catholics on the other did emerge, and the more recent characters in this book reflect a greater diversity of Christian backgrounds and understanding of that faith.

By the eighteenth century, Yorkshire was one of the great centres of the Industrial Revolution and the West Riding began to grow in importance. The growth of the Church in that part of Yorkshire depended on the work of committed individuals at least as much as the institution, and this is picked up in the story of Henry Venn. We will also learn something of the variety of Christian groups through the stories of Richard Oastler, and Polly and Smith Wigglesworth. By the middle of the nineteenth century York became a major centre of the railway boom, and this enabled the development of other industries, including chocolate and confectionery. York remained a particularly important religious centre as the base for the Archbishop of York while during the twentieth century, like other cities, it saw the growth of new forms of Christian communities. Although he was a Church of England minister, David Watson's life illustrates the development of new forms of church which continues to the present day.

Finally, in gaining a bigger picture of the Church in this region it is important to recognize the difficult challenges that industrialization and the growth of large cities have posed. Some places, like Middlesbrough, had a strong church life, partly because so much of the growth came through the immigration of Irish Catholics. In other cities, such as Hull and Sheffield, the Church across denominations struggled to connect with the new working populations, and even now church life is weaker in some Yorkshire cities than in other parts of the country. The challenge for the Church to connect with ever more diverse groups of people is still there and calls for courage and imagination. It may be that in some small way inspiration for the future may be drawn from the example of God's Own People in the past.

Timeline

This timeline is intended to list some key events described in this guide. A full list of the lives of even the people described would require many more pages. Many dates are approximate, especially before about 1200.

306   Constantine declared Roman Emperor at York
313   Edict of Milan brings official toleration of Christianity in the Roman Empire
314   First record of a bishop of York

410   Roman rule in Britain abandoned

593   Bernicia and Deira united as Northumbria through marriage

627   Baptism of Edwin and Hilda by Paulinus at York
633   Death of Edwin in battle (born around 585)
644   Death of Paulinus
647   Death of Ethelburga (born around 605)
657   Whitby monastery founded by Hilda
664   Synod of Whitby
664   Death of Cedd at Lastingham
672   Death of Chad
680   Death of Hilda (born around 614)

709   Death of Wilfrid (born around 634)
721   Death of John of Beverley (born around 640)
731   Publication of Bede's *Ecclesiastical History*
735   Bishop of York elevated to Archbishop
793   First Viking raid on Lindisfarne

804   Death of Alcuin of York (born 735)

1066   Norman invasion of England
1069   Harrying of the North (especially Yorkshire)
1069   Selby Abbey founded by Abbot Benedict

1132	Rievaulx Abbey founded by Abbot William and Walter Espec
	Fountains Abbey founded by Thurstan
1140	Death of Thurstan of York (born around 1070)
1167	Death of Aelred at Rievaulx (born 1110)
1218	Death of Robert Flower of Knaresborough (born around 1160)
1349	Death of Richard Rolle at Hampole (born around 1300)
1433	Death of John Thornton
1536	Pilgrimage of Grace
1537	Death of Robert Aske, executed in York (born 1500)
1538–9	Dissolution of the larger monasteries including those at Rievaulx, Fountains, Selby and Whitby
1586	Death of Margaret Clitherow, executed in York (born 1553)
1645	Death of Mary Ward in York (born 1585)
1686	Bar Convent, York set up to continue Mary Ward's work
1791	Death of John Wesley (born 1703)
1797	Death of Henry Venn (born 1725)
1807	Abolition of the slave trade in the British Empire
1833	Death of William Wilberforce (born 1759)
1840s	First Industrial Revolution at its height; railway mania
1850s	The start of the modern chocolate business
1869	Death of Richard Oastler (born 1789)
1925	Death of Joseph Rowntree (born 1836)
1947	Death of Smith Wigglesworth (born 1859)
1984	Death of David Watson (born 1933)
1994	Death of Ted Wickham (born 1911)

DAY 1

Whitby and the Yorkshire Moors:
Early days for the Christian faith

Our opening day is focused on some of the deeply committed women and men who rooted Christianity into the Yorkshire landscape, especially by establishing monastic communities on the coast and the Yorkshire Moors. We begin with Hilda, the founder of the original Whitby Abbey in 657 and its abbess for nearly thirty years. She was a remarkable woman who was held in high esteem by many church leaders, from Aidan to Cuthbert. She hosted the Synod of Whitby which determined that the Church in Northumbria would follow Roman and continental practices in dating Easter, and enabled the Church to move on beyond the associated controversy. The story of Caedmon, keeper of the animals turned hymn writer, is entwined with Hilda's.

We also hear the story of the brothers Cedd and Chad, who were trained on Lindisfarne, set up their own monastery at Lastingham and were missionaries in several kingdoms of Anglo-Saxon England. Our final person today is Aelred, the energetic abbot of Rievaulx Abbey, who was a nationally important diplomat, and was in charge of a large monastery in the twelfth century, while also writing a number of very significant books. Besides brief descriptions of the places important in the lives of these people, several other possible pilgrimage sites are mentioned at the end of today's chapter. This pattern is followed for each day.

People

Hilda (614–81)

Hilda is an excellent first saint for this book: she was one of the earliest Christian leaders in Yorkshire and is a reminder that women have had significant roles in the Church. I feel a personal connection in that one of my grandmothers was called Hilda, even though I didn't know anything about the saint for many years, and I am writing this in St Hilda's Vicarage in York! Her significance is such that she has been claimed as an exemplar both by those who support the ordination of women and those who oppose it. Virtually everything we know about her is in two chapters of Bede's *Ecclesiastical History* (Book 4, chapters 23 and 24), along with some scanty archaeological material. She is best known for founding the double monastery at Whitby, a place that drew on the Roman and Irish Celtic traditions of Christianity.

Hilda (or Hild) was born in 614, to the ruling royal family of Deira, roughly modern-day Yorkshire. She was a great-niece of King Edwin, who became *bretwalda* (high king) of the English in the 620s. (His story is included on Day 3.) Her father was Hereric, nephew to Edwin, and her mother Breguswith. Hilda is thought to mean "maid of war, or battle". At the time of her birth Northumbria was ruled by Ethelfrith of the royal family of Bernicia, based in Bamburgh. It was a tough period; her father was in exile when she was very young, and he later died from poisoning.

When she was a child her family regained the kingdom of Northumbria and her great-uncle Edwin became king in 616. It seems that he ruled as a pagan for the first years of his reign, but converted to Christianity after a long process involving his marriage to princess Ethelberga of Kent, a series of violent episodes, and much reflection with Bishop Paulinus. He was baptized at York at Easter 627, along with many of his household, including Hilda, now aged thirteen.

Just a few years later, in 633, Edwin was killed in battle, leaving the queen and other members of the family to be taken south by Paulinus for protection. We are not told what happened to Hilda, but it is possible she also went south. Her older sister, Hereswith, had married Ethelhere, the king of the East Anglians, and another possibility is that Hilda went to the court there. Given that she was now nineteen, her apparently unmarried status may suggest that she was already keen to pursue the religious life.

We are not told anything more about her until 647. That year, at the age of thirty-three, she responded to a call to the monastic life. Hilda first went to East Anglia and intended to go to a French convent, at Chelles near Paris, to join her widowed sister. However, Aidan of Lindisfarne called her back to Northumbria, and she was given a hide of land on the north bank of the Wear, enough to establish a household. Forming a small community, she stayed there for a year.

Following the departure of its founding abbess, she was next called to lead the monastery at Hartlepool, a daughter house of Lindisfarne, and she gave it a firm foundation during her nine years there. According to Bede, Aidan and other devout men admired her wisdom and would also visit to offer their guidance and affectionate support.

In 657 Hilda founded the double monastery at Whitby at the prompting of King Oswy. Up to this point the most important monastery in Northumbria had been Lindisfarne, itself founded at the instigation of King Oswald. Following the assassination of Oswin, King of Deira, Oswy needed to assert his authority over the southern kingdom. He turned to Hilda as the existing pre-eminent leader of a monastery in that part of Northumbria. Her royal pedigree ensured her recognition socially and her piety and wisdom ensured her spiritual recognition.

The early monasteries were simple wooden affairs, unlike the stone ruins we see today. Whitby was a double monastery: communities of men and of women lived alongside each other and came together for meals and for prayers. This may have had some link to Irish monasticism; many of their foundations might be described as Christian villages, housing men, women and children. However, the strongest link was to other double monasteries in northern Gaul, or Francia, where they were something of a speciality. Among them was Chelles where Hilda's sister Hereswith had gone. In fact Bede records that from 640 many prospective nuns went to Francia because there were so few monasteries in England. Hereswith and Hilda were part of a wider movement. As happened elsewhere, Whitby became a centre of learning, the mother monastery of a network of smaller foundations, such as Hackness and Lastingham. This was a co-operative venture between the secular ruler and religious leaders.

Bede emphasizes the way that Whitby followed the example of the early Church in four ways, all of them dependent on Hilda's own devotion and example:

First, Hilda "taught the observance of righteousness, mercy, purity and other virtues, but especially of peace and charity". The emphasis on peace and charity seems to reflect Bede's own undertsanding that these qualities were not automatically or easily achieved in a closed community. At her death Hilda urged her community to keep the "gospel peace amongst themselves". For this was a community of people of both low and the highest social standings, and in life outside the monastery the hierarchy was very strict.

Secondly, strongly reminiscent of the early Church was their attitude to possessions, a feature picked up from Aidan's example, as well as a reflection on the church described in Acts 2:44–45: "no one was rich, no one was needy, for everything was held in common, and nothing was considered to be anyone's personal possessions" (*Ecclesiastical History*, Book 4, chapter 23).

Thirdly, Hilda was consulted by ordinary folk and nobles for advice, "so great was her prudence". Again, there was a democratic flavour to the comment, indicating her willingness and ability to speak with all classes of society.

Fourthly, part of the eclipsing of Lindisfarne at this period was the way in which she established Whitby as a place of learning. This meant the "thorough study of the Scriptures", something close to Bede's own heart, and engaging in good works.

Thus Hilda trained many nuns, priests and no less than five bishops, including Wilfrid (see Day 5). Besides her learning, a significant part of her influence was the result of her personal example of holy living, an influence which spread beyond her own communities to many others who heard accounts of her life.

A story from the last year of her life illustrates her gift of encouragement.

Caedmon was a keeper of animals for the monastery who discovered a gift for writing poetry. One evening there was a feast at which the harp was being passed round for each person to sing. Caedmon always left early as he was unable to sing, but this time, after fulfilling his duties in the stables, and settling for sleep, he had a dream. A man called to him to sing—to sing of creation, in the English language, beginning:

> Praise we the Fashioner now of Heaven's fabric
> The majesty of his might and his mind's wisdom.

In the morning Caedmon added further verses and took them to his superior, the reeve, or estate manager, who took him to Hilda herself. With others, she agreed this was a gift from God, and she encouraged Caedmon to take monastic vows in order to use this gift in writing songs for the community. According to Bede, he wrote songs on the whole story of the Bible from creation, through the history of Israel, the life, death and resurrection of Jesus, and the final judgement. Sadly none of these have survived.

Hilda became seriously ill in 674 when, aged sixty, she was racked by a "burning fever". However, she continued to teach and lead her community until her death in 680. Her saintly life was confirmed for her contemporaries by a vision granted to a nun called Begu, who lived at a daughter house of Whitby called Hackness. Whilst at rest she heard in her mind the bell used when any of the sisters died. Then she saw a great light, which she perceived as the soul of Hilda ascending to heaven. The next day it was found to have been the very time at which Hilda had died. In this way Hilda's sanctity was authenticated.

In Hilda we see a woman who did not deny her background in a royal family but worked with the needs of her society to work out how Christianity would both fit into their culture and re-shape it. Her gifts of wisdom, encouragement and teaching all played a part in this. Like others, Bede admired her evident holiness, evident in her lifestyle and teaching. Her life illustrates the importance of those who can bring together opposing factions: how might her spirit of reconciliation work out in our own times?

Cedd (died 664) and Chad (died 672)
Cedd was the oldest and Chad the youngest of four Anglo-Saxon brothers, born in Northumbria and in the first generation of English monks and priests. Their lives show how Christian holiness was developed and

lived out in demanding times. The brothers—Cedd, Cynibil, Caelin and Chad—all trained on Holy Island under Aidan's leadership. Most unusually all became priests, and Cedd and Chad were also bishops.

After Aidan's death Cedd was chosen by King Oswy to be one of four priests on a mission in 653 to the Mercians, preaching and baptizing. This proved successful and he was quickly sent on a second mission, this time to Essex, after the conversion of Sigbert, king of the East Saxons.

This clearly went well for in 654 he was recalled to Holy Island and consecrated by Bishop Finan as Bishop of the East Saxons. Returning to Essex, probably by sea, Cedd founded several churches, where he baptized converts, and two monasteries at Bradwell-on-Sea and at Tilbury. Bede emphasizes the difficulty of founding monasteries among "untutored folk", but Cedd tried to teach them monastic discipline.

Cedd continued to travel back to Northumbria to preach and he renewed his friendship with King Ethelwald, the sub-king of Deira, and the son of King Oswald. Their friendship was assisted by Cedd's brother Caelin, who was the king's chaplain. The king asked Cedd to found a monastery on his own lands as a place for his own burial. Cedd chose a place in the remote hills (as it seemed to Bede, living in a monastery well-connected by sea routes) and he founded his third monastery at Lastingham on the southern edge of the North York Moors.

Rather helpfully for us, Bede gives more detail of the spiritual preparation in the founding of this monastery than any other. So we learn that Cedd deliberately chose a place more suitable for robbers and wild beasts in order to purify it for God. He achieved this by praying and fasting on the site throughout Lent. He fasted each day until evening (except for Sundays), and even then ate only a little bread, and egg and watered milk. This was how he had been trained on Holy Island: before any monastery or church was built the site was dedicated in prayer and fasting.

Cedd was a prominent person at the Synod of Whitby, as a supporter of the Irish side. However, he was clearly trusted by all for he was the key interpreter for both parties. As a result of the meeting he accepted the Roman argument over the dating of Easter, and is the one person named as doing so, though many other people did too. His leadership in this matter is thus made obvious, but sadly it was not to last for long as he caught and died from the plague when visiting Lastingham and was buried there.

He was succeeded by his brother Chad as abbot, and the monastery survived the attack of plague. After Cedd's death about thirty of his monks came from Essex to be with their founder in life and death, and all but one died of the plague very soon after their arrival. Later, when life was more settled, a stone church was built to commemorate Cedd's holy life, and his encouragement of others to live in the same way.

Just a year after the plague Chad was chosen to be Bishop of York. Wilfrid had previously been chosen for the office, but he had travelled to France for his consecration and the king had grown impatient. However, Chad's own consecration was complicated by the lack of an Archbishop of Canterbury and he turned to other bishops, not universally recognized, for his consecration. This was not valid in the eyes of the new Archbishop of Canterbury, Theodore, and he appointed Wilfrid as Bishop of York in place of Chad. At this point Chad retired to the monastery at Lastingham.

As Bede tells it, Chad's humility clearly impressed Theodore and since the Mercian people needed a new bishop, Theodore arranged for Chad's consecration. Chad was following in the footsteps of his brother some sixteen years earlier and travelled the kingdom preaching the good news of Christ from his new monastic community in Lichfield in the kingdom of Mercia. He died there in 672, surrounded by his fellow monks.

Cedd and Chad undoubtedly drew strength for their ministry from their practice of prayer and fasting. Having a community of like-minded monks was important to them wherever they went. Lastingham had a special place in their affections for its remoteness, associated with the wild and desert places of the Bible, where God could be encountered in a deeper way and where people wrestled with their inner demons in pursuit of holiness. Cedd and Chad's commitment to community life and their personal humility remain inspiring.

Aelred (1110–67)
Aelred's oldest friend Simon was dying. He was in the infirmary and nothing could be done except to make him as comfortable as possible. The love and prayers of the whole monastery were with him until the inevitable end came.

Friendship is always tested by hard events and the twelfth-century abbot Aelred knew that better than most. Against the advice of many of his monastic predecessors he emphasized the value of making friends in the monastery. He knew it would lead to loss and bereavement, but he also believed that the benefits of having close friends with whom we can share our deepest feelings and concerns made it worthwhile. He even went so far as to add to the phrase from the Bible "God is love", another—"God is friendship".

Aelred's commitment to friendship was the more remarkable for he lived in dangerous times: he was born about 1110, not long after the Norman Conquest and the terror of the Harrying of the North. He saw the flourishing of monastic life but also lived through the turmoil of the dreadful civil war between King Stephen and his cousin Matilda. During that sad period he managed to develop a successful community of monks at Rievaulx, nestling in a valley on the south-west edge of the North York Moors, near Helmsley.

By the end of his life Aelred was known throughout England and beyond. He had doubled the number of monks and lay brothers at Rievaulx to 600, developed the buildings and founded other monasteries elsewhere, and he was a regular correspondent of King Henry II and many bishops and leading figures of his day.

Aelred was born at Hexham in Northumberland, into a family of priests who for several generations had tended the shrine of St Cuthbert at Durham. His father was from the last generation of married priests, for reforms which included an insistence on celibate clergy were underway. These reforms originated with Pope Gregory VII in Rome, but were brought to England via the Norman Conquest.

Aelred was brought up with connections to the aristocratic families of Northumbria and Scotland, and spent time at the Scottish court of King David. He was clearly well liked, trusted and capable. Even as a young man he was given some responsibility in the court for arranging feasts and entertainments, and this trust was extended to more important matters.

However, for all his success he was not entirely happy and wanted a clearer sense of his calling in life. It was at this time, in 1134, when aged about twenty-four, that he was sent on King David's business to York to meet Archbishop Thurstan (see Day 5). Thurstan had recently supported the founding of strict Cistercian abbeys at both Rievaulx and Fountains and it seems likely that Aelred heard talk of these foundations during his visit. Like the much earlier monastery at Lastingham these were deliberately founded in wild places to promote a connection with God. It had the additional benefit over time of repairing some of the devastation caused by the Harrying of the North several decades previously.

On his return journey to Scotland Aelred stayed at Helmsley Castle with Walter Espec. Espec was the patron of Rievaulx and had given land for it just two years earlier. So Aelred took the opportunity to look at the new temporary monastic buildings there. After animated discussion with his companions, the next day Aelred offered himself at the gates of Rievaulx to join the monastic life. He had left the relative luxury and ease of courtly life and entered into one of severe discipline and hard physical work. But he had clearly found his spiritual vocation, and he quickly made his mark as a reliable and wise member of the community.

Aged thirty-two, Aelred was sent by the abbot to Rome to represent him in legal wrangles over the election of Thurstan's successor as Archbishop of York. On the way he met the leading Cistercian monk of his day, Bernard of Clairvaux, an important man who was to remember Aelred later.

On his return to Rievaulx he was given the key post of novice master, especially important as large numbers of men were applying to join the abbey. Among his duties was giving talks on the monastic life, and eventually he wrote these up on the orders of Bernard of Clairvaux into the book called *Mirror of Charity*, partly as a justification of the severity of the Cistercian rule of life. After a few months as novice master Aelred was sent to start a new monastery, as the first abbot of a new Cistercian house at Revesby, Lincolnshire. He did this so well that just four years later (1147) he was called back to Rievaulx, as the third abbot.

The monastery at Rievaulx was said to be 300 strong when Aelred was elected abbot, and it doubled in size in his time. In addition, there were many daughter houses, spread between southern Scotland, Yorkshire and down to Bedfordshire, which required his attention and visitations. Further arduous travel was necessary to attend the General Chapters at Citeaux in France. Only in his later years, after nearly twenty years of rigorous work, and when ill health took hold, did he accept the need to delegate some of these responsibilities.

His commitment to friendship and his common sense made him a confidante of kings, including Henry II, and of bishops and nobles, including the Bishop of London and the Earl of Leicester. Three hundred of his letters were preserved until the fifteenth century.

All this outside work was additional to the daily prayers of the monastery (the seven monastic offices) and his duties in the abbey, overseeing major expansion and rebuilding at Rievaulx itself. The nave of the church, the cloisters, the infirmary (where Aelred's friend Simon died) and buildings for the tanning vats were all built during Aelred's time. When wandering these vast buildings, we can imagine the huge amount of work required to build all of it by hand, and the energy of abbot Aelred in bringing it to pass.

By 1157, aged forty-seven, he was in poor health and he was allowed to live and pray in the infirmary, where he had a small cell built. The ruins, where Aelred took time to pray, to write and to converse with his monks, can still be seen. During this time he wrote several important reflections on the spiritual life, including his *Pastoral Prayer* and *Spiritual Friendship*. He was able to look back on a life of both activity and contemplative prayer, and he helpfully explored the complexities of loving ourselves, our neighbours and God.

In the last four years of his life he seems to have adopted an even more austere lifestyle, spending much more time in prayer and vigils, and forgetting his meals at times. He died on 12 January 1167, in the company of his monks at Rievaulx.

Friendship was important to Aelred. He said: "Scarcely any happiness whatever can exist among humanity without friendship." He was convinced that friendship sprang from God, and that it is part of our nature as created by God. He knew the sadness of losing friends; he knew the problems and limitations of love and friendship within communities, but he was confident that with God's help these could be overcome.

Places

Whitby

Whitby Abbey was founded in 657 by Hilda as a royal monastery on behalf of her kinsman Oswy. As we saw, under Hilda the monastery became known as a place of learning and godly living. After Hilda's death in 680 her successor was Aelffled, daughter of King Oswy and his queen Eanfled, a cousin of Hilda. Although having a second royal abbess meant that Whitby was still important, its pre-eminent position was lost, and Lindisfarne recovered its leading position, under Cuthbert, before and after his death.

The abbey was destroyed in a Viking raid of 867 and the site largely deserted until renewal in the eleventh century. Pilgrims then began to return, and a new church was needed in the twelfth century to cope with the numbers. These are the ruins still visible, which survived the Reformation because they were useful to ships entering the harbour.

English Heritage now cares for the buildings and provides excellent interpretation boards and audio tours. They are inclined to over-emphasize the importance of the Synod of Whitby (it was not that crucial in the story of the Church in Western Europe), but there is a full and interesting account of the history of the site from the time of Hilda to the present day.

- <https://www.english-heritage.org.uk/visit/places/whitby-abbey>

St Mary's Church has a breathtaking and windy setting on the cliff top overlooking the estuary of the River Esk one way and the ruins of the abbey the other. The favoured way of reaching it is up the 199 steps from the old port, though a gentler walk is possible by road from the abbey car park. The building dates back to the eleventh century and is wonderfully eccentric; it seems that items have been added over the generations but rarely removed. It is particularly notable for its box pews, triple-decker pulpit, Elizabethan Communion table, and even two nineteenth-century ear-trumpets! Appropriately it feels like being in an old wooden ship and on a windy day that can be very comforting. I remember sheltering there for a service on a wet Sunday in August, grateful that our young children could play and dry off in peace in one of the big box pews—God's Own People in Whitby are still very welcoming!

Lastingham

Lastingham is a delightful village on the southern edge of the North York Moors. There is an old church on the site of Cedd's monastery. The present building dates from after the time of the Norman Conquest and includes an atmospheric crypt built in the eleventh century over the place where Cedd was believed to have been buried.

- <https://www.lastinghamparishchurch.org.uk/>

Rievaulx Abbey

Rievaulx Abbey was built by the Cistercian monks in the twelfth century in a secluded valley about two miles from the market town of Helmsley. Its most important period spiritually came under its third abbot, Aelred. Today these are some of the most complete monastic ruins in northern England, a spectacular sight in the deep and narrow valley.

The castle ruins at Helmsley, where Aelred first heard of the monastery, are well worth a visit, and then you can take a delightful walk through the woods to Rievalux Abbey, following in the steps of Aelred all those years ago. Wandering the picturesque ruins of Rievaulx we can still marvel at what faith and friendship can achieve, even in dangerous times.

- <https://www.english-heritage.org.uk/visit/places/rievaulx-abbey>
- <https://www.english-heritage.org.uk/visit/places/helmsley-castle>

Prayer

Gracious God
You inspired Hilda and Caedmon, Cedd
    and Chad, Aelred and his friends
to praise your name
to live in community
to show love to God's people

and to train women and men in the ways of holy living.
You inspired countless pilgrims on arduous journeys
to find your guidance.
Inspire us in our turn through the lives of your people
that we may praise your name
live in godly community
show your love
and live in holiness.

Practicalities

Whitby

Whitby is reached via a scenic road (A171) over the North York Moors. Whitby is signed off the A19 at the A174. On approaching the town follow signs for the Abbey, where there is ample parking. There is also a rail service, with mainline trains from Middlesbrough down the Esk Valley, and a tourist service from Pickering on the North York Moors Railway. You may wish to walk one of the newer pilgrimage routes to Whitby: St Hilda's Way which goes inland to visit churches associated with Hilda across 40 miles of the North York Moors into Whitby.

- <https://johneckersley.wordpress.com/sthilda/>

The Way of St Hild pilgrimage route follows the coast from Hartlepool to Whitby, in a reminder of Hilda's own journey.

- <https://britishpilgrimage.org/portfolio/way-of-st-hild/>

Refreshments and toilets are readily available at the Abbey and in the town. Whitby is famous for its fish and chips!

Lastingham

Lastingham is somewhat off the beaten track, requiring a journey through narrow country lanes off the A170. It is a beautiful village set in a narrow valley, with views from various footpaths in the vicinity. There are walking routes up onto the moors from the village.

Rievaulx

The Abbey is just over two miles north of Helmsley, on a minor road off the B1257. It is signed, though you have to be careful not to go onto Rievaulx Terrace by mistake. It can be reached on foot by following the Cleveland Way from Helmsley. Refreshments are available at the Abbey café and at numerous places in Helmsley.

Other sites

There are many other pilgrimage sites on the North York Moors, among them:

Egton Bridge

About eight miles west of Whitby, the village of Egton Bridge was the birthplace of Nicholas Postgate. He was brought up as a Roman Catholic when this was still illegal and became a priest serving in the locality, before being executed in York in 1679, one of the very last Roman Catholic martyrs in England. The Roman Catholic church of St Hedda's contains his relics.

Hackness

One of Hilda's outlying monasteries was founded here not far from Scarborough. St Peter's Church is a welcoming place which has material from Anglo-Saxon times to the present day, though the remains of the original abbey are no longer visible. The church is nearly always open in daylight hours and worth a visit if you are travelling down the coast from Whitby in the direction of Scarborough.

Pickering

Pickering Church can be visited by travelling over the moors from Whitby on the A171. It has one of the best preserved sets of medieval wall paintings in the country. They have recently been restored and are shown to great effect. Pickering is also a good place to find lunch!

- <http://www.pickeringchurch.com/>

Kirkdale
St Gregory's Minster, Kirkdale, is a very rare example of an English church with an inscription commemorating a Viking benefactor. The inscription is on a sundial over the door, dating from before the Norman Conquest. It is found just north of the A170, and a visit can be combined with a trip to Lastingham. The church is open daily from 9.30am to 6pm (or dusk, if earlier).

- <https://www.kirkdalechurches.org.uk/st-gregors-kirkdale/>

Byland Abbey
These spectacular ruins are said to include the inspiration for the great Rose Window at York Minster. The monks who built this abbey in the twelfth century were part of the Cistercian movement, along with the community at Rievaulx. The community was also connected with Archbishop Thurstan and later with forming a new monastery at Jervaulx (see Day 5).

- <https://www.english-heritage.org.uk/visit/places/byland-abbey>

Osmotherley
Osmotherley is an attractive village on the western edge of the Moors. The Church of England building, which is on a Saxon site, is a beautiful building, while the nearby market cross is said to have been used several times by John Wesley as a place to preach. Just outside the village the Shrine of Our Lady of Mount Grace, the Diocesan Shrine for the Catholic Diocese of Middlesbrough, is a peaceful place with wonderful views. Below the village Mount Grace Priory is one of only nine Carthusian priories founded in this country and is the best preserved.

- <https://www.english-heritage.org.uk/visit/places/
  mount-grace-priory/>

Osmotherley is also home to Osmotherley Friends Meeting House, which is a traditional stone building, erected in 1690 or 1723. It is thought that George Fox may have visited the village in the late-seventeenth century.

Recently a 134-mile pilgrimage route has been created linking together seven abbeys—Kirkstall, Fountains (Day 5), Byland, Rievaulx, Lastingham, Rosedale and Whitby.

- <https://britishpilgrimage.org/portfolio/
  yorkshire-dales-abbey-way/>

DAY 2

The Yorkshire Coast and Wolds: Supporting the downtrodden

The second day of our pilgrimage explores the old East Riding of Yorkshire, which takes in the southern section of the Yorkshire coast, the Yorkshire Wolds and the often-overlooked city of Hull. Our first character is John of Beverley, one of the earliest bishops of York, a man with deep roots in the East Riding and a real concern for the poor and needy. In terms of geography it is a small step to William Wilberforce, who was born in Hull, though it is a big step in history to the early stages of the British Empire when William Wilberforce and many others fought against the slave trade. The final person on our pilgrimage today may seem a little unusual: Robert Aske was a lawyer who led a rebellion against the king of England. His story, together with others in this book, is a reminder of the continuing significance of the Roman Catholic faith in many parts of Yorkshire.

The East Riding tended to be the most prosperous area of the county before the Industrial Revolution, and so there are still many larger churches from the medieval period. Two of the largest in England are Beverley Minster and Hull Minster, each associated with one of God's people described here. So along the way we will visit Beverley, Hull and the village of Aughton where Aske was born and brought up. Other places in the East Riding which can be part of a longer pilgrimage visit include Bridlington, Holderness, Pocklington and Howden.

People

John of Beverley (c.640–721)

John of Beverley was one of five men who went on to become bishops after being trained for the priesthood by Hilda at Whitby. The stories we have of him tell us he was highly respected, much loved and lived as a follower of Jesus by caring for the whole range of people around him. The rest is sketchy but perhaps that doesn't matter: how we live and put our faith into action counts far more than our personal history.

John's early life is not well recorded. Later traditions from the time of his canonization as a saint (in 1037) claim that he was born to aristocratic parents at Harpham, near Driffield in East Yorkshire, possibly around 640. One of the few churches dedicated to him is still there. Traditions also says that he was educated at Canterbury under Archbishop Theodore. We are confident that he was at Whitby with Hilda, because the monk and historian Bede tells us this: he knew John personally.

John was Bishop of Hexham (687–706) and in that post he ordained Bede deacon at eighteen (c.691) and priest at twenty-nine (c.702). As bishop, John took what opportunities he could to pray and reflect with a few companions, especially during Lent, but he also insisted that they cared for a poor person during their stay not far from Hexham. On one occasion they took in a dumb youth who lived nearby and made him his own little hut. On the second Sunday of Lent bishop John asked the boy to come to him and gave the gift of speech to this young man: first he made the sign of the cross on his tongue and then he encouraged the boy to say "yes", followed by the letters of the alphabet, and other basic sounds. After a couple of days he was able to talk well and could share his thoughts with them for the first time. Bede starts by describing this as a miracle, though the way he tells the story sounds like an early form of speech therapy.

As much as being astounded by any miracle, I am struck by John's patience with the young man. He is willing to keep going through slow progress, until eventually the lad could speak and express himself. John backed it up with an offer to join his household, and although it was declined by the young man, we can sense the joy this cure produced.

Whatever you make of miracles, it is clear that Bede believed there were plenty of reliable reports of them performed through John's prayers and actions. From the time that John was Bishop of York (706–14 or 718) Bede selected another four miracles that he performed in the region around Beverley, all of them in life-threatening situations. They involve a woman who had been acutely ill for many weeks; a nun with a swollen and wounded arm after it had been bled, which sounds like a very bad infection; a serving boy who was completely paralysed; and a priest who had cracked his skull falling from his horse after some foolish galloping. In each case Bede takes care to explain how he knows the story; however we interpret the details I am confident that we have an accurate report of the recovery of these people.

Bringing healing and care is clearly important in itself, but just as significant is the range of people that John met and healed: a young man; a nun; the wife of a thane (one of the local lords); the servant boy of another thane; and one of his clergy. This man of God was out and about amongst the people in his region, and they felt they could approach him, whether high or low born, male or female, lay or religious.

In his sixties John retired from his role as Bishop of York to a monastery he had founded at In-Derawuda, meaning "in the wood of Deira", where he died in 721. His tomb became a site of pilgrimage associated with healing, and the town of Beverley grew up around the church. His canonization in 1037 strengthened Beverley as a pilgrimage centre and the gifts of pilgrims enabled the building of the impressive church still there.

It seems unlikely that the historical John would have wanted this kind of attention. The impression we get from Bede is of a humble man who was open to showing the love of God to all kinds of people. Personally, I am both attracted to and challenged by John's openness to other people, in all sorts of conditions—what do you make of his story?

William Wilberforce (1759–1833)

William Wilberforce is rightly best remembered for his long campaign, with many partners, for the abolition of the slave trade in the British Empire, but he was a man who worked hard on many causes, political and religious. He is a good example of how a rich and well-connected man made use of his advantages in life for the benefit of others, and all based on his Christian faith. And unlike many of the other holy people we celebrate he was not a monk or a priest, but a family man, with all the ups and downs that implies!

Wilberforce was born on 24 August 1759 in Hull, the only son of Robert, a wealthy merchant, and his wife Elizabeth. He began his formal education at Hull Grammar School where he was taught by Isaac Milner, who was to be a great religious influence and mentor.

Sadly his father died when William was only eight years old. His mother then became ill and sent him to London to live with his aunt and uncle, Hannah and William Wilberforce, for two years.

Hannah and William were devout Evangelical Methodists. They took William to church regularly, where he heard the preaching of George Whitefield and John Wesley. William's mother, Elizabeth, was worried about his exposure to such a strong religious influence, and when she was well again she called him back home to Hull. From there he was sent to board at Pocklington Grammar School, where he did well at Latin, English and History.

At seventeen he went to St John's College, Cambridge, where he began a lasting friendship with the future prime minister, William Pitt the Younger. Politics was their passion and in 1780, at twenty-one, the youngest age at which one could be so elected, William was returned to Parliament for Hull, then a "rotten borough", a parliamentary seat with a very small and unrepresentative electorate. Four years later he was again returned to Parliament, this time for the county seat of Yorkshire which was large and populous, and which therefore required an expensive election contest. The advantage was that the election, being more democratic, conferred a greater legitimacy on the two Members whom the county returned to Parliament.

Wilberforce's early years in Parliament were not untypical for a young backbencher. He was noted for his eloquence, charm and wit, attributes no doubt enhanced by his considerable wealth, but he did not involve himself at first with any great causes. In 1785 he travelled in Europe with his mother, sister and his former teacher Isaac Milner. Through conversation and studying religious writing together Wilberforce had a relatively sudden conversion to evangelical Christianity. His cheerful nature remained but from then onwards he approached politics from a position of strict Christian morality.

Soon after his conversion he met the ex-slave trader John Newton for the first time and thus began his interest in the abolition of the slave trade, on the basis of his Christian convictions. The abolitionist Thomas Clarkson also had an enormous influence on Wilberforce, and he was persuaded to lobby for the abolition of the slave trade. For eighteen years he regularly introduced anti-slavery motions in Parliament, despite being repeatedly rebuffed. In the early 1790s there was a boycott of sugar organized across the country, which motivated many people, though it did not lead immediately to success on the anti-slavery campaign.

By 1792 Wilberforce had left Hull and moved to Clapham in London to be closer to his work in Westminster. Within the Clapham community he found friends who shared his interests in religion and politics, the "Clapham Sect" (see Henry Venn, Day 6). They actively supported the anti-slavery abolitionists in raising public awareness by producing pamphlets and books and organizing rallies and petitions. Living in the same location meant the possibility of sharing ideas, prayer and worship, which strengthened their commitment, essential in the demanding task they had set themselves.

Failure in 1797 to get a Bill passed for even gradual abolition of trading led many people to abandon the cause, but Wilberforce was not one of them. However, he did take up other causes more fully, including founding the Bible Society and the RSPCA. He worked with the reformer, Hannah More, in the Association for the Better Observance of Sunday. Its goal was to provide all children with regular education in reading, personal hygiene and religion. He was also instrumental in encouraging Christian missionaries to go to India. In all, Wilberforce led or supported sixty-nine societies.

In 1797 he married Barbara Ann Spooner, and they went on to have six children. Wilberforce was a loving and devoted husband and father and was proud that three of his sons became clergymen; one became a bishop and one an archdeacon.

Political changes in the new century helped the campaign to abolish the slave trade and Wilberforce published an influential tract in 1806. In 1807, the slave trade was finally abolished, but this did not free those who were already slaves. Wilberforce believed in the abolition of slavery itself, but realized this would take time and many more battles. At first he sought to work with allies but they would not allow him to speak publicly of his belief. From 1815 he became impatient with this approach, and despite the deterioration of his health he campaigned openly and as widely as he could manage. Wilberforce retired from politics in 1825 and died on 29 July 1833, three days after the Bill to free slaves in the British Empire passed through the House of Commons.

As a politician, it is clear that Wilberforce understood Christian mission included challenging injustice as well as evangelism. He knew that prayer and campaigning went together. His faith gave him the inspiration to act and kept him going through many disappointments. As he put it in 1804 after yet another defeat in the House of Commons, "When men are devoid of religion, I see that they are not to be relied on."

His prayer then became: "Lord, I am in great troubles, insurmountable by me, but to thee slight and inconsiderable. Look upon me with compassion and mercy . . . ."

As a layman he took prayer and Bible study very seriously. Although he remained an Anglican, the influence of the Methodists was seen here:

> This perpetual hurry of business and company ruins me in soul if not in body. More solitude and earlier hours! I suspect I have been allotting habitually too little time to religious exercises, as private devotion and religious meditation, Scripture-reading, etc. Hence I am lean and cold and hard.
>
> I had better allot two hours or an hour and a half daily. I have been keeping too late hours, and hence have had but a hurried half hour in a morning to myself. Surely the experience of all good men confirms the proposition that without a due measure of private devotions the soul will grow lean.*

What a challenge! He kept setting this kind of goal for himself, and failing, because he was so caught up in campaigning. So before we all

---

* Robert I. Wilberforce, Samuel Wilberforce, *The Life of William Wilberforce: In Five Volumes* (London: John Murray, 1839), p. 207.

flagellate ourselves perhaps we should remember that even Wilberforce could not maintain this standard!

Finally, as a family man, he was committed to reading and praying with his wife and children. Despite all the demands upon his time he knew that a significant part of God's call to him, God's mission for him if you will, was to be as good a husband and father as he could.

Robert Aske (1500–37)

Robert Aske may seem an unconventional choice for a book on saints: he was a lawyer who led a rebellion against the king and ended up being executed for treason. So why include him? I do so because his motivation for rebelling seems to have been genuinely religious in the best sense. Like many other people of his time, especially in the north of England, he was convinced that the closure of monasteries under Henry VIII and the changes to worship in parish churches were causing harm to people. Despite the bad reputation of some monasteries many of them were still places where ordinary people could find food when hungry, medical help, the possibility of some education for their children and a source of spiritual comfort.

Even though he was significant in leading what he called the Pilgrimage of Grace and came close to overthrowing the rule of Henry VIII, we know surprisingly little about Aske, except for the nine months of the rebellion in 1536–37. He was born in about 1500, the third son of Sir Robert Aske of Aughton near Selby, a second cousin of the Earl of Northumberland, and was distantly related to Queen Jane Seymour. We know that he had only one eye—it even features in a version of the Mouldwarp prophecies of the time—but we have no information on why that was.

As a young man Aske went to London to study law at the prestigious Gray's Inn, one of the four Inns of Court. Besides a thorough education in law and other subjects he also formed connections with prominent people, links which could be expected to last a lifetime. The training he received developed his skills in analyzing complex documents and in persuading other people of his point of view through accomplished rhetoric.

On graduating he seems to have divided his time between clients in London and elsewhere and the family home in Aughton. He didn't marry but lived with his elder brother John, who was head of the family by 1536. At this time the Dissolution of the Monasteries was causing considerable anguish in many parts of the country. Aske found himself caught up in an initial rising, in Lincolnshire: he was travelling with three of his nephews from Yorkshire to London in October 1536 when they were forced by a group of Lincolnshire rebels to swear an oath supporting the rising. Their journey to London was halted and Aske was almost immediately seen as a leading figure. Presumably he already knew of the rebellion and was sympathetic to the cause.

Over the coming days Aske repeatedly crossed the River Humber, using the ferry that ran close to the site of the modern-day Humber Bridge. He worked hard to bring order to a number of small, local uprisings on both sides of the Humber because he wanted to see how the king would respond to a petition already sent from Lincolnshire. He saw rebellion as a very last resort. In the event he was unable to control what was happening in the area around Aughton, and he took on leadership of these groups on 11 October, the eve of St Wilfrid's Day, then a significant occasion of celebration in Yorkshire.

Other uprisings were occurring all over the north of England and within days—16 October—Aske led an army of perhaps 5,000 men to York, where the mayor surrendered the city, with the provisos that no harm would be done to the citizens and that all food was bought at the going rate. Most of the army stayed outside the city walls, camping around crosses brought from their own parish churches. Aske stayed in the city for two days and wrote what he called "The Oath of the Honourable Men". It began:

> Ye shall not enter into this our Pilgrimage of Grace for the Commonwealth, but only for the love that ye do bear unto Almighty God, his faith, and to Holy Church militant and the maintenance thereof, to the preservation of the king's person and his issue, to the purifying of the nobility and to expulse all the villein blood and evil counsellors against the commonwealth from his Grace . . . .

It went on to state that they entered into the Pilgrimage not for personal gain but for the restoring of the Church and the ending of heresy.

Within a week, Hull fell to a rebel group, while Aske marched south to Pontefract Castle, which surrendered to his army. Groups from all over the north swelled the rebel numbers to about 40,000. Against them was a much smaller king's army, of about 8,000. Its commander, the Duke of Norfolk, played for time, eventually negotiating a truce with Aske; both sides were uncertain of the eventual outcome of the rebellion. Fearing the size of the rebel army Norfolk promised to take their demands to the king, to call a parliament in Yorkshire to hear their grievances and to offer a general pardon. The Pilgrimage of Grace effectively ended on 7 December, after negotiations at Doncaster. Aske and the rebels rather naively believed what they had been promised, though nothing had been put in writing. That a highly trained and competent lawyer like Aske accepted this is perhaps evidence of his own good faith and a belief that the rebellion had succeeded without bloodshed.

Henry did not see it that way. Privately he was furious with Norfolk. To gain some control he invited Aske to spend Christmas at Greenwich Palace with him. During this time Aske wrote a detailed account of the uprising at the king's request, and it provides a detailed source of the events and also evidence of Aske's own gullibility. Returning home in January, Aske found that the common people did not trust the king's words and were ready to rebel again. Aske travelled to Beverley and was able to calm the situation there. Elsewhere right across the North groups were forming for another rebellion without Aske's support, in an attempt to ensure that the king honoured his agreements of the year before.

Once again the king sent the Duke of Norfolk to put down the uprisings, ordering him to "act without pity". This he did. Being more fully prepared this time, rebels were hunted down, trials were held and rebel leaders' bodies were left hanging in trees and on gallows as a sign of the king's displeasure.

Aske himself was imprisoned in the Tower of London for interrogation. As part of this he had to answer 107 formal questions, some of which he put in writing. Although accused of treason, even now he answered straightforwardly, seemingly unable to hide the truth. His brother, Christopher, gave evidence against him, while his older brother, John, was forced to sit on the jury. He was sent to York where, on 12 July 1537, he was tied to a hurdle and dragged through the streets to Clifford's Tower. There he was hanged, though unusually the king showed some mercy in ordering that he be pronounced dead before being drawn and quartered. His body was left to hang in chains from the castle walls as a warning to other potential rebels.

Robert Aske comes across as a generally honourable and honest man, who believed the king to be surrounded by evil advisers, most notably Thomas Cromwell. He clearly had strong leadership qualities recognized from the beginning by the rebel groups and he was able to hold them together under immense pressure from the king's forces. His weakness, his naiveté, was to believe that Henry VIII and the Duke of Norfolk were as honourable as he was. It is a reminder of how difficult it can be for devout Christians to live out their faith in the political sphere. His story, admittedly in more violent circumstances, makes an interesting contrast to that of Wilberforce, who managed to maintain his integrity while being realistic about the shortcomings and duplicity of many with whom he had to deal. As Jesus put it, "I am sending you out like sheep into the midst of wolves; so be wise as serpents and innocent as doves" (Matthew 10:16).

Places

Beverley

Today the market town of Beverley is a thriving and pleasant place to visit, retaining many independent shops in its centre alongside the well-known ones. As well as two of the most significant parish churches in England, Beverley still has a large number of Georgian streets and buildings, the fifteenth-century North Bar, attractive cafes and pubs, and a well-known racecourse.

Our pilgrimage visit is focused on Beverley Minster, where John of Beverley is buried and commemorated, and at the other end of the town centre, St Mary's Church, itself a very fine building which was the original parish church and the place of worship for many of the crafts guilds in the town.

- <https://beverleyminster.org.uk/>
- <https://stmarysbeverley.org/>

Although the minster is the resting place of John of Beverley nothing remains from the monastery or church of his time. His simple tomb is at the east end of the nave: at the time of writing this there are plans to emphasize its significance. He is also commemorated by a large eighteenth-century statue to the right of the south door. Another statue of John is to be found amongst those of other saints, including St Hilda and St Bede, in the reredos, behind the high altar. This is visible across the church when entering by the main door on the north side. In the south transept John's story is told in a delightful series of thirty-four tapestries made in 1961.

The building as a whole is much acclaimed for the beauty and harmony with which it combines three Gothic styles—Early English, Decorated and Perpendicular. As with any church of this size and age, the details of its construction are complex. Information is available on the church's website and in the church itself. One of the newest features is worth looking out for in the context of this book: a new window and artwork celebrating pilgrimage were installed in 2004 in the retro choir at the east end of the building. It offers a lovely space in which to take time to reflect and pray.

Returning to the busy streets of the town, and avoiding the temptations of shops, restaurants and pubs, head north along Highgate for the half mile walk to St Mary's Church, which is on Hengate. This too is a fine Gothic church, with a splendid west end, a fascinating sequence of paintings of kings of England on the chancel ceiling and twenty-eight wonderful misericords in the choir. These include an elephant and castle, and apes, foxes and monkeys representing doctors, priests and bishops of the time. Another unusual feature on the north side of the nave is the so-called "minstrels' capital", featuring five musicians with eccentric costumes and haircuts. Again, there are many more features to explore.

As with many towns and cities, the prosperous centre of Beverley can disguise the fact that for many people in the town life is much tougher. God's people in these two churches and the others in Beverley share a concern to meet the practical and spiritual needs of their neighbours.

Why not take a moment in St Michael's Chapel—entering past the White Rabbit of Alice in Wonderland fame—to remember the people of the town before God?

Hull

The city of Hull used to be one of the UK's most important ports and so was targeted in the Second World War. It suffered badly from multiple bombing raids and has struggled to recover. The massive decline in the fishing industry in the 1970s was a further blow, and the city is still seeking to re-establish its identity. Becoming City of Culture for the UK in 2017 has been a significant boost to the city's profile and led to some significant investments. One place to visit on this pilgrimage is the original parish church of Kingston upon Hull, Hull Holy Trinity, which was renamed Hull Minster by Archbishop John Sentamu at a ceremony in May 2017. The church has been undergoing a wonderful transformation in the past few years, not just as a building, but also as a Christian community serving the city.

In connection with our pilgrimage Hull Minster is notable as the place where William Wilberforce was baptized; you can see the font which is still in regular use. In the church there are many memorials, including to the many Hull lives lost at sea. The Triple Trawler Tragedy of 1968, which claimed fifty-eight crewmen within three weeks, is one of the most poignant events commemorated here. This is a good place to give thanks not just for the work of Wilberforce and other abolitionists, but also for those many unsung heroes who risked their lives on the high seas.

- <https://hullminster.org/>

The other place most associated with Wilberforce is Wilberforce House, where he was born. It is now a free museum with displays about his life, and also about the slave trade and the efforts to end it.

- <https://www.hcandl.co.uk/museums-and-galleries/ wilberforce-house/wilberforce-house>

Aughton

Aughton is a tiny village now, very much off the beaten track. The church that Robert Aske knew is still there and makes for a peaceful and interesting visit. There are several family connections, including brass memorials of Sir Richard Aske and his wife Margaret from the fifteenth century. On the outside of the tower, on the south side, there is an intriguing design of a heraldic shield and the inscription: "Christofer le second filz de Robert Ask chr oblier ne doy, Ao Di 1536".

This may be translated as: "Christopher, the second son of Robert Aske, knight, ought not to forget the year of our Lord 1536".

The Robert Aske mentioned here is the father of John, Robert and Christopher. The tower was rebuilt by Christopher after 1536, and this inscription is thought by some to be a roundabout way of acknowledging and even regretting his part in his brother's trial and execution. One further Aske link is the carving of a newt on the south side of the tower: aske is an alternative Middle English word for newt!

Beyond the east end of the church, across the grassy track and then a small moat, is Aughton Hall. The earlier buildings here were owned by the Aske family until about 1645. There is no public access to the present complex, but it can be viewed from the track leading to the church. Along with the remains of a Norman motte and bailey castle to the north of the church this is an impressive collection of old buildings, made even more atmospheric when winter floods cover the surrounding fields.

Prayer

God of the downtrodden,
you raise up people with the fire within them to care for others.
We thank you for John of Beverley, William Wilberforce,
    Robert Aske and those who worked with them
in caring for those in need
in lifting up the downtrodden
in working for justice for those beaten down by the powerful.
Give us grace, strength and fire
to seek a better world for all God's people.

Practicalities

Beverley
Beverley is set in the beautiful Yorkshire Wolds and is easily reached by road on the A1079 between Hull and York and the A164 between the Humber Bridge and Driffield. It is also on the train line between Hull and Scarborough.

There is a new pilgrimage route between Beverley and Bridlington, taking in older routes which medieval pilgrims would have used.

- <https://britishpilgrimage.org/portfolio/ beverley-to-bridlington/>

Hull
Hull is easily reached by road and rail connections from several directions.

The Deep in Hull is the starting point for the Wilberforce Way, a longer pilgrimage walk of sixty miles, from Hull to York. It goes via Beverley and includes other places of worship, not necessarily connected with Wilberforce.

- <https://www.ldwa.org.uk/ldp/members/show_path. php?path_name=Wilberforce+Way>

Aughton
From Hull, Aughton can be reached via the A1079 and A613, or the A63/ M62, and then north from Howden on the B1228 to York. From York the route is via the A19 to Escrick and then the A163 and B1228. Aughton is signed off the B1228, together with a sign for an historic church. Once in the village drive to the end of the "no through road", to The Old Coach House and Aughton Hall. There is a short walk on a grassy track to the church.

Other places

Bridlington

Bridlington Priory was founded in 1113 as a house of Augustinian canons. It was well endowed and produced scholars and musicians from its early days. In the fourteenth century the then prior, Prior John, made such an impact with his prayers, study and kindness that he was canonized as St John of Bridlington. The monastic community was dissolved at the Reformation, but the church was retained as the parish church, and today is still a lively place of prayer and pilgrimage. It is open most days—check the website for details.

- <http://bridlingtonpriory.co.uk>

Patrington, South Holderness

The Holderness area, east of Hull, can seem quite remote but it has some wonderful churches and history, a reminder that it was once very prosperous. The best of the churches is St Patrick's, Patrington. It is a beautifully proportioned, largely fourteenth-century building. It is likely that the de Patrington family of masons were responsible for most of the work. Their leading member, Robert, went on to be master mason at York Minster in 1369, and it is thought (locally at least) that some of the designs of capitals and bosses at Patrington were later used in York Minster.

- <http://www.stpatrickspatrington.org.uk/>

Pocklington

Pocklington is a small market town, just off the A1079 between Hull and York. There is an eight-and-a-half-mile walk from Warter to Pocklington which takes in a few places associated with the Pilgrimage of Grace, where the rebels gathered as they made their way to York. The church at Pocklington is impressive and mentions a possible link to Paulinus, preaching and baptizing nearby in the 620s. It is also a stop on the Wilberforce Way.

- <http://www.top10trails.com/yorkshire-wolds-way/4>
- <http://www.pocklingtongroupofchurches.org/pocklington.html>

Howden

Just off the M62, Howden boasts the impressive remains of a medieval minster church. The east end is now in ruins, but other parts of the church are still in use and can be visited. Much of this area belonged to the Bishops of Durham in the Middle Ages, and they built a Bishop's Manor as well as the church, hence the grandeur in a small town. John of Howden was one of the early leaders of the Church in the thirteenth century and may be the author of various spiritual writings which influenced Richard Rolle (see Day 7). Howden was one of the places which strongly supported the Pilgrimage of Grace.

- <https://www.english-heritage.org.uk/visit/places/howden-minster/>

York: Minster and St Michael-le-Belfrey: The ancient centre

On this pilgrimage I have devoted two days to the city of York because of the depth and richness of its religious and political history. Even two days does not allow time to include all the well-known examples of God's People with significant connections to the city, so if you are visiting do look out for people and places that I have not mentioned. I have given a few links on finding more information for other historic churches in York at the end of the material for Day 4.

York scores highly in national surveys of the best towns in which to live. Because of its history and many attractions it is visited by millions of people from all over the world. It celebrates its many layers of history from the Romans to today, via Angles, Vikings, Normans and even industrialization—railways and chocolate come to mind! It has been the formal capital of the north of England for long periods of time, and has been the base of the second archbishopric in England since the post was created in 735.

This rich history means that we can encounter a variety of Christians from many centuries and many parts of the Church. Day 3 reflects the more public and upbeat side of York, with its focus on the Minster and the ancient centre of the city. The first stories are those of the makers of the first minster on this site, Edwin and his court, followed by that of Alcuin, one of the leading scholars of his day, and then, representing countless other builders, the master glazier, John Thornton. We end with the inspiring twentieth-century story of David Watson, based across the road at St Michael-le-Belfrey. Day 4 explores some of the complexities, diversity and sheer nastiness of the wider story of York.

People

Makers of the first Minster
Edwin of Northumbria (c.586–633) and Ethelburga of Kent and York (c.605–47)
Paulinus the Bishop (died 644) and James the Deacon (died after 671)
The first church on the site of the present-day York Minster was a hastily erected wooden building for baptisms at Easter in 627. The story behind this involves many people and is a reminder that the mention of God's Own People in this book is to be understood as a collective reference, not an individual one. None of the people achieved what they did on their own, not even the hermits, so it is good to emphasize these four people together, beginning with Edwin.

Edwin was the Anglo-Saxon king of Northumbria from 616 to 633, ruling from York. According to Bede he became the most powerful English ruler of his day and was the first Christian king of Northumbria. In truth it is likely that Edwin's conversion to Christianity was as much a political act as a religious one. Nonetheless Bede describes him as a thoughtful and reflective man, who took time on his own to think things through. Perhaps somewhere in the complexity of being an Anglo-Saxon warrior-king he did find some peace from God through Jesus Christ.

Not much is known about his family background but we do know he was born around 585, a son of King Aelle of Deira, that his sister Acha was married to Ethelfrith, king of Bernicia, and that another sibling was the parent of Hereric, Hilda's father. Edwin fled into exile when his father was killed, and there are confused records of where he went and what he did. His story comes into focus during his time at the court of King Raedwald of East Anglia, who saw him as a protégé. In 616, after a battle against Ethelfrith, Raedwald installed Edwin as king of Northumbria. Later Edwin conquered part of Wales and was recognized as overlord by all the other English rulers except the king of Kent.

If he had any Christian faith at this time, it was not made public (once again there are divergent records on this). It is more likely that he ruled as a pagan for the first years of his reign, though Bede interpreted Edwin's success as due to God's favour. The first mission to convert the Northumbrians came about because Edwin wanted to make an alliance with the powerful Kentish kingdom, in support of his bid to be overlord. His first wife had died, and he took the opportunity to link himself with Kent through marriage. However, their marriage in 625 was only granted on the condition that Ethelburga and her household were allowed to continue practising Christianity in Northumbria, and that Edwin himself consider converting to Christianity. Ethelburga was accompanied by her Christian advisers and her chaplain, Bishop Paulinus, who himself had originally arrived in England in 601, in the second wave of missionaries from Italy.

Edwin remained cautious about the Christian faith, and Paulinus made little headway in his efforts to convert him. Then, a suicide mission was sent to kill Edwin by Cuichelm, the king of the West Saxons, on Easter Day 626. Edwin was protected by his favourite counsellor, Lilla, who placed his body in the way of a poisoned dagger. After wounding the king and killing another man the would-be assassin was killed. The same day the queen gave birth prematurely but Paulinus prayed for them and she and the child survived. Paulinus interpreted the events as evidence of the Christian God's protection, and Edwin was sufficiently convinced to have his new-born daughter, Eanfled, baptized along with twelve of her household on the following Pentecost.

Edwin himself held back from baptism until he had defeated Cuichelm. Having proved this God in battle, he continued to mull over whether or not to accept the Christian faith. Bede tells us that Edwin would often sit alone turning things over in his inmost heart. The process of conversion was drawn out and involved letters from the Pope to Edwin himself and to Queen Ethelburga, Edwin being reminded of a vision he had had earlier, and finally a meeting of the council of his principal advisers, the Witan or Witenagemot. Their agreement was guaranteed by the stirring words of Coifu, high priest of their ancestral gods, who believed that the Christian faith offered more certainty about the afterlife. He backed up his words by destroying idols at a village east of York, now called Goodmanham.

A wooden church was quickly built in York and Edwin was baptized there the following Easter in 627, along with many of his household, including Hilda. Bede tells us that Edwin ordered a stone church to be built on the site, though he died before it was completed. His head was later buried there in a porch dedicated to Pope Gregory.

After his baptism Edwin used his influence over the bishops, the construction of Christian centres and the deployment of clergy, as means of control in his kingdom. Bede saw this as a golden age in which there was peace, and people could walk from one side of the kingdom to the other without fear. Paulinus was able to take advantage of this relatively peaceful time to preach and to baptize across a wide area, from south of the River Humber to the far north at the royal estate of Yeavering, on the north side of the Cheviot Hills.

But just a few years later, in 633, Edwin was killed at the battle of Hatfield (South Yorkshire), fighting the forces of Cadwalla of Gwynedd and Penda of Mercia. One of Edwin's adult sons was killed and the other captured by Penda, whilst the queen, his younger children by Ethelburga and his grandson, and possibly Hilda, were taken south by Paulinus for protection. Paulinus was made Bishop of Rochester, where he worked until his death in 644. At the same time Queen Ethelburga founded a nunnery of Lyminge, near Folkestone, which she led until her death in 647. Like Hilda's monastery at Whitby archaeological research seems to suggest this was also a double monastery for men as well as women.

And what of James the Deacon? He had assisted Paulinus in his tours of preaching and baptizing, but he stayed behind in 633 to care for the church at York. He provided continuity as a Christian community slowly developed in York and the surrounding countryside. He was very knowledgeable about church music and was able to teach the people to sing—once peace was restored. He seems to have lived for another thirty years or so, and Bede writes very warmly of him as "a man of great energy and repute in Christ's Church".

The lives of these makers of the first minster in York are very different from our own: the level of violence and insecurity was beyond anything in modern-day Britain. Lives truly were nasty, brutish and short for nearly everyone. Most people held some kind of religious belief, though there was clearly competition between the different faiths. As present-day pilgrims, we can be grateful for the early attempts to develop a Christian society. Convincing warring tribes to follow Jesus the Prince of Peace took time, but it had to begin somewhere, and this was a key period in that process. Do you feel able to give thanks for these early people of faith, even while acknowledging their flaws and shortcomings?

Alcuin of York (735–804)

Alcuin was a scholar, poet, teacher and abbot born in York around 735, who went on to have an international career under the greatest ruler of his time in Western Europe. He was sent to the cathedral school, under the first Archbishop of York, Ecgbert, and his successor Ethelbert. He was a quick learner, said to know the Psalms by the age of eleven. He spent more than forty years in the school and the Minster, becoming a monk and teacher. Around 778 he was ordained as a deacon and also became the master of the school at York, which still exists as St Peter's School.

In 781, he was sent to Rome to petition the Pope on behalf of the archbishop. On his return journey at Parma he met the king of the Franks, Charles the Great, known as Charlemagne. Charlemagne recognized in Alcuin a scholar who could help him achieve a renaissance of learning and reform of the Church, and subsequently enabled him to join his court in 786. He returned to Northumbria for three years from 790–93, but he was unable to make any impact on the violence associated with the king. As a result, he went back to Charlemagne's court and later became a leading scholar in the palace school at Aachen. There he established a great library, including some books from York. Alcuin was a superb teacher and scholar. He had the ability to guide others through what he saw as "golden whirlpools of spiritual meaning", and to inspire them to rise to even greater intellectual heights. The example of Alcuin's work at Aachen encouraged a wider movement starting schools of learning in monasteries and cathedrals.

In 796 Alcuin became abbot of St Martin's monastery at Tours, where he established another school and library, continuing his ministry of education and encouragement to the end of his life. He died at Tours in 804.

Alcuin wrote many poems, one of which celebrates York:

> My heart is set to praise my home
> And briefly tell the ancient cradling
> Of York's famed city through the charms of verse.
> It was a Roman army built it first,
> High-walled and towered, and made the native tribes
> Of Britain allied partners in the task –
> For then a prosperous Britain rightly bore

The rule of Rome whose sceptre ruled the world –
To be a merchant-town of land and sea,
A mighty stronghold for their governors,
An Empire's pride and terror to its foes,
A haven for the ships from distant ports
Across the ocean, where the sailor hastes
To cast his rope ashore and stay to rest.
The city is watered by the fish-rich Ouse
Which flows past flowery plains on every side;
And hills and forests beautify the earth
And make a lovely dwelling-place, whose health
And richness soon will fill it full of men.
The best of realms and people round came there
In hope of gain, to seek in that rich earth
For riches, there to make both home and gain.*

In his final years he was a prolific letter-writer and produced texts to assist in teaching Christian faith. He was very concerned that faith was genuinely held: "What avails baptism without faith?" and "a man can be forced into baptism but not into belief" as he wrote to two missionary colleagues (Alcuin, *Letters*, 164).

Alcuin is an example and encouragement to anyone seeking to share their faith through teaching. He was much appreciated by his pupils in the long decades he taught in the school at York, and in his final years he was able to influence kings and rulers across a significant part of Western Europe. Not many of us can hope to achieve the same, but his life and faith can inspire us to pass on our faith to the next generation. Why not take a moment to pray for someone who needs to grow or even come to faith in Jesus?

A Maker of the later Minster: John Thornton, glazier (active in York 1405–33)

The great buildings like York Minster that we see today were designed and built by people, nearly all of them unknown to us. Unusually, we do know

---

*   Patrick Ottaway, *Archaeology in British Towns: From the Emperor Claudius to the Black Death* (London: Routledge, 2005), p. 122.

that the master glazier for York Minster in the early fifteenth century was called John Thornton. He is included to represent countless other designers and workers from past centuries, even though we know nothing of his or their faith. What we do have is Thornton's masterpiece of the Great East Window of the Minster, telling the stories of the beginning and end of things in the Bible, from the Books of Genesis and the Apocalypse or Revelation.

John Thornton was from Coventry and was a skilled glass painter in his hometown, where he may have been an assistant to his father. He was given the contract to glaze the East Window of York Minster in 1405, probably because the Archbishop, Richard le Scrope, and the funder, Walter Skirlaw, had both been bishops of Coventry and presumably knew his work. The window was completed in just three years and Thornton received £56 for his work. His role was primarily that of designer, leading the team of glassmakers, designers and builders who installed the painted glass.

Thornton was made a freeman of York in 1410, but went back to live in Coventry by 1413. He seems to have lived mostly in that city though records in York show that he received some further payment from the Dean and Chapter in 1433. And that is all we know about the man behind one of the greatest works of art in England. It was produced for the glory of God and to tell the story of God as it was understood at the time. The anonymity of most makers of the Minster and the other churches we have from the medieval period may be surprising in our own day, but they were confident they were known to God. That was what counted to them, and it can still be the basis of our own spiritual security.

David Watson (1933–84)
David Watson, who arrived in York in 1965, grew a large congregation from almost nothing, first at St Cuthbert's and then at St Michael-le-Belfrey. His own spiritual journey led him from his father's commitment to Christian Science, via atheism to evangelicalism in the Church of England. Discovering a form of spiritual renewal in the charismatic movement in the 1960s was crucial to his own development and his ability to grow a church. As his experience grew, Watson broadened his appreciation of other Christian traditions and worked for reconciliation in the Church and beyond.

David Watson was born in 1933 in army quarters in Catterick, but his earliest years were spent in north-west India where his father was stationed. The family returned to England in 1937, but his father would be away for months at a time. It was while his father was in India in 1943 that he caught bronchial pneumonia, and true to his own faith as a Christian Scientist, he refused treatment. Sadly he died. David's mother had him baptized and confirmed in the Church of England, and he attended services. However, he could not understand what was going on and tried other religious paths for a time. After school, on National Service, he joined the Army, still a nominal Anglican, but finding no joy in it he became an atheist.

After his two years in the Army he went to Cambridge University in 1954, to study mathematics. But he switched to read moral sciences instead, which included philosophy, psychology and logic. In the first week he found himself at a tea party run by a Christian group. There he heard a compelling talk on Christianity by a young clergyman called John Collins. He was invited to have breakfast with Collins the next day and by the following evening he had committed his life to God. He was nurtured in his faith by the Christian Union, led by David Shepherd, then the England cricket captain. Later Watson switched his studies to theology, though he struggled with some (not all!) of the approaches taken by his lecturers. Crucially he became involved with the "Bash camps" for public schoolboys. Watson later wrote in his autobiography: "Undoubtedly the most formative influence on my faith during the five years at Cambridge was my involvement with . . . 'Bash camps.' . . . It was the best possible training I could receive." He began to grow in his knowledge of his faith, putting it into practice with a range of people, and learning how to speak of Christ in ways which connected with them.

He was ordained deacon in 1959, starting work among the dock workers of Gillingham, Kent, with John Collins as his vicar and David MacInnes as a fellow curate. Here he learned to develop his evangelistic gifts in a very down-to-earth context. A contrasting second curacy took him back to Cambridge, to the Round Church, where the vicar was Mark Ruston. It was at this time that Watson became less satisfied with what he felt were rather dry services and Bible studies. He sought the experience of baptism in the Holy Spirit and began to speak in tongues.

In his autobiography he spells out the highs and lows of this development, and the pressure put on him to renounce this experience which was regarded with suspicion by many of his fellow conservative evangelicals.

It was also while at Cambridge that he met Anne, a nurse, who became his wife. His openness about his shortcomings as a husband is both moving and disarming—it does not sound an easy marriage, with David endlessly inviting his contacts to their cramped flat or disappearing to take yet another university mission somewhere. He had terrible asthma at times and needed Anne's skills as a nurse to help him through. This and the times he was away led them both to experience depression.

They both believed that they were called in 1965 to leave Cambridge and head north, namely to York, and Watson became Curate-in-Charge of St Cuthbert's. It was attended by no more than twelve at any service, and was twelve months away from redundancy. In a ministry of prayer and Bible study, tears and heartache, they saw the congregation grow, not least by providing a spiritual home for the students at the new and secular university. Eight years later the congregation had outgrown St Cuthbert's and its extra rooms and they moved to St Michael-le-Belfrey, where the congregations continued to grow. Among his methods, a commitment to living simply in shared households was very important. Besides the example it gave of Christian living it also released people to assist in developing creativity in worship and in the missions that Watson led in York and in many other places. Eventually he led over sixty festivals on five continents.

In the 1970s Watson also developed his commitment to reconciliation and ecumenism, notably in Northern Ireland. When he held town-wide festivals, he insisted that they were ecumenical, a desire which arose from his involvement in charismatic renewal. In 1977 at the National Evangelical Anglican Conference he described the Reformation as "one of the greatest tragedies that ever happened to the Church". Today many Christians may understand what he meant, but at the time many fellow evangelicals thought he had gone too far. He continued to stand by what he had said, believing that reform had been needed and if it had been taken up by the Church institutions in the sixteenth century the body of Christ would not have been split.

In 1980, in what turned out to be the final phase of his life, he met the founder of the Vineyard church movement, John Wimber from the

USA. Watson was one of the first people to welcome Wimber to the UK, which led to a new impetus and direction for charismatic renewal in this country. As pressure continued on him to travel the world, and battling the asthma which he had had all his adult life, he and his family left St Michael-le-Belfrey in 1982 for London. Shortly after that he was diagnosed with cancer. Having spoken honestly about other difficulties in his life he recorded his own struggles with the disease, suffering more generally, and the pressure on his faith in his last book, *Fear No Evil*. Despite much prayer for healing from around the world he died on 18 February 1984.

In his autobiography Watson described his vision as evangelism, renewal and reconciliation. He lived this out both at the local level and through missions. Even now there are many people who remember him with affection and gratitude. His legacy continues in their lives and in the church community at St Michael-le-Belfrey, which is still a centre for renewal. His convictions can be summed up at the end of what was probably his most significant book, *Discipleship*:

> In view of the urgency of the times, we are to live lives that honour Christ, heal the wounds within his body, and that hastened the coming of the day of God. . . . Christ looks for disciples who are unashamed of him, of obedience to his word, united in his love and filled with his Spirit.*

Places

York Minster
York Minster is widely regarded as one of the greatest and largest cathedrals in northern Europe, and the present building took about 400 years to complete, starting in 1080. Before you enter you might like to spot the statue of Constantine the Great on the south side of the building, and near it a column from the period of the Roman Empire. They are reminders of the part York played in that era: it was the main northern

---

* David Watson, *Discipleship* (London: Hodder and Stoughton, 1981), p. 258.

base for the Roman army during its occupation of Britain and also the place where Constantine was declared Emperor by his troops in 306. That link is strengthened when you realize that the church is almost certainly built on top of the *principia*, the headquarters of the Roman fortress.

Visitors enter at the west end, under a massive wall of stone, one of the windiest places in York, it seems to me. If you are attending a service of worship entry is free. On entering, my first impression is the sheer scale of the building and only over time do the details begin to take shape. Going on a guided tour is recommended as the guides are able to bring to life the stories behind the architecture. The museum in the crypt, accessed by steps on the right-hand side more than halfway down the church, tells the long history of the site, beginning with the Romans and Anglo-Saxons.

On the other side of the church, the chapter house is reached down a corridor. This is still used for official meetings and other events. Do look at the carvings over each stone seat: there are animals, human faces, and a few jokes tucked in by medieval stone masons. In connection with the story of John Thornton the highlight of a visit is undoubtedly the Great East Window, at the opposite end to the entrance. There is plenty of space to linger and enjoy—perhaps with binoculars—the colourful windows which pick out the stories in the Bible of the beginning and the end, creation and judgement. Over them all is God the Father, set in the heavenly realm, amongst angels, prophets and other key figures. Immediately below are twenty-seven figures from the Old Testament and then no less than eighty-one scenes from the Apocalypse (the Book of Revelation). At the bottom is a single row of nine historical figures, including Bishop Walter Skirlaw, who seems to have paid for the work.

A good website for further information is:

- <http://www.yorkglazierstrust.org/about-us/case-studies/ york-minster-great-east-window/>

There are numerous chapels for personal prayer—my own favourite is the crypt at the east end, near the Great East Window. It is an intimate space which contrasts with the massive scale of the building as a whole and provides a place in which you can be still and quiet.

A straightforward guide to the building of the minster can be downloaded:

- <http://yorkcivictrust.co.uk/wp-content/uploads/2017/06/York-Minster_-How-the-Minster-was-Built-YorkWalks.pdf>

St Michael-le-Belfrey and St Cuthbert's House of Prayer

St Michael-le-Belfrey is the only church in York that was built in the sixteenth century, replacing an earlier medieval church that was so unsafe that parishioners were afraid to enter the building for services. The church may be named after the minster bell tower or belfrey which stood on the site before the church was built. Guy Fawkes, one of the Gunpowder Plot conspirators, was born nearby in Petergate and was baptized in this church in 1570. The martyrdom of Thomas Becket is recorded in the east window, a rare survival as Henry VIII ordered all images of St Thomas to be destroyed in 1538. Apart from the gallery added in 1785 and the west front rebuilt in 1867, the building in 2020 remains an unusually intact example of a sixteenth-century church.

At the time of writing there are ambitious and imaginative proposals to re-order the interior and possibly the entrance, in keeping with both the church's history and present needs. Multi-million-pound gifts have been offered and the church community is actively working on a scheme. When you read this it is possible that the building will be closed for the re-ordering work, or looking further ahead (summer 2022?) re-opened to welcome visitors and pilgrims.

St Cuthbert's House of Prayer is based in the ancient church of St Cuthbert's where David Watson began his ministry in York. It is now dedicated for the use of private and corporate prayer, generally in informal style. It is one of the oldest church buildings in York and nestles just inside the city walls. Its website provides details of when it is open and the events hosted there.

- <https://www.yhop.co.uk/>

Prayer

Gracious God
you come to us as mighty Lord and suffering servant
you are king of kings and vulnerable child
In this place of magnificence and grandeur
may we find both your strength and your humility.
We thank you for those who went before us
to see your church built in stone and in people.
As we draw on your humble strength
may your church be transformed in love,
    compassion and service of others.

Practicalities

York

York is easily reached by road and rail connections and offers a multitude of places to stay. Linked to this book you might consider staying at the Bar Convent, where Mary Ward is commemorated. Her story is told on the next day:

- <https://www.bar-convent.org.uk/accommodation.htm>

For those wanting to connect with Paulinus there is a new pilgrimage route from Todmorden to York, joining the sites of Paulinus Crosses, thought to have been erected wherever Paulinus had preached:

- <https://britishpilgrimage.org/portfolio/paulinus-way/>.

Other places

See Day 4

DAY 4

York City: A shadow side

York was the capital of the north of England for many years, most obviously after the Norman Conquest, and so its history reflects the concerns of successive monarchs, powerful nobles, civil war and unrest. We have already heard of the trial of Robert Aske in York and of his body left to rot in chains on the castle walls (Day 2). At other times traitors were beheaded and their heads left on Micklegate Bar as a warning to others.

Religious intolerance, often connected to political concerns, was pronounced after the English Reformation in the 1530s. The story of Margaret Clitherow reminds us of the personal devotion and commitment to the "old religion", that is Roman Catholicism, felt by many in this area. She was just one of the most well-known examples of persecution leading to martyrdom. In the following century religion was still highly contested, and Mary Ward had to set up her society for women in secrecy. As York developed during the Industrial Revolution, it became a place of marked social deprivation. As in a number of other places, positive change was brought about by people with a Nonconformist religious background. In York the lead was taken by the chocolate manufacturing family Rowntree, most especially Joseph, and his story illustrates the impact that a determined (and well-connected!) individual can make.

At the end of today's material there are some suggested links to other people and places in the story of York.

People

Margaret Clitherow (1553–86)

The small crowd on Ouse Bridge was grim-faced and determined. They had a job to do and, however distasteful, someone had to do it for the sake of queen and country. Coming towards them, dressed only in a white gown reminiscent of a nun's habit, was their pregnant neighbour, Margaret Clitherow. She struggled through the busy streets, with gifts of money for the onlookers who pressed in on all sides. In her mind she was going to martyrdom for the sake of her God, whatever the authorities thought of her. York in the 1580s was a city still divided by the Reformation conflict between Catholics and Protestants, but the city fathers had fallen in line with Queen Elizabeth as the threat of a Spanish invasion grew. Margaret had chosen to suffer the hideous death of being pressed, or crushed, because her conscience demanded it of her for "the love of the Lord Jesus".

Her upbringing was conventional enough: Margaret was born in York in 1553 (though some books say 1556), one of five children of Thomas and Jane Middleton. Her father was sheriff of the city in 1564, a prominent businessman and a churchwarden of St Martin's Church in Coney Street. Assuming she was born in 1553, she would have some early experience of Roman Catholic worship in the reign of Mary I. This changed back to a Protestant form in the early years of Elizabeth I's reign after 1558. Margaret's father died in 1567 when she was just fourteen. In 1571, at the age of eighteen, she married John Clitherow, a widower and a wealthy butcher living in the Shambles. John already had two sons, William and Thomas; Margaret and John were to have several children together, Henry, Anne, and possibly two more. As one of the leading men in York, John worshipped in the Church of England and continued to do so throughout his life, though his own brother, William, became a Roman Catholic priest. Margaret was expected to attend church with her husband and initially did so.

The circumstances of her conversion to Roman Catholicism are not entirely clear: it occurred in 1573 or 74, apparently through the influence of Dorothy Vavasour, the wife of a prominent Catholic doctor, Thomas Vavasour. The Vavasours were deeply committed Catholics, hosting illegal Masses in their home, and eventually both died in separate prisons. Margaret seems to have been inspired by the devotion and suffering of Catholic priests and laypeople for their cause.

This was a particularly difficult development for Margaret's husband, who was responsible for reporting Catholic worshippers to the authorities in the parish, but it seems he paid Margaret's fines for not attending church services. However, her commitment to her faith deepened, no doubt supported by the Vavasours and other Catholics in the city, such as the master of Archbishop Holgate's School, John Fletcher. As a result, she appeared on lists of recusants—the legal term for people who refused to attend the Church of England services—beginning in June 1576. She was summoned before the High Commission twice in 1578, in 1579, and in 1580, all for recusancy. In October 1580 she was sent to the York Castle prison for her refusal to take an oath of allegiance or change her religion. Released from prison for childbirth in April 1581, she spent about two years out of jail before returning, in March 1583, after yet another conviction for recusancy. In all she was imprisoned for about twenty months. While in prison, she accepted the poor food as an aid to prayer and fasting, and she learned to read Latin so she could assist with Catholic services.

Her fervour was not dampened by prison. She educated her children as Catholics; she started to provide hiding places for priests in her house in the Shambles and on occasion she hosted Mass. Between 1582 and 1583 five priests were put to death at Tyburn on Knavesmire, the site of the present-day York Racecourse, and when not in prison Margaret would make a night-time pilgrimage to the gallows. During those visits, which were not known to her husband, her later biographer wrote of her approaching "barefoot . . . and kneeling on her bare knees ever under the gallows" until her companions urged her to go home.

During this period she sent her older son, Henry, to the English College, relocated in France, to train for the Catholic priesthood. Her husband was summoned by the authorities to explain why his son had gone abroad, and in March 1586 the Clitherow house was searched for priests. The secret room and a cupboard for ritual items were discovered after a terrified boy revealed its location and admitted that priests had been in the house.

The government of Queen Elizabeth was deeply concerned about a possible invasion led by the Catholic king of Spain and so had passed harsh laws against priests and those who supported them. Under the 1585 *Act against Jesuits, Seminary Priests and such other like Disobedient Persons*, it was treason to be a priest or Jesuit, and anyone who sheltered priests could be punished by death. This was the charge against Margaret Clitherow, though it was unusual for the sentence of death to be carried out.

Margaret was arrested on 10 March 1586 and appeared in court on 14 March. Her trial took place in York Guildhall, or rather that was the intention. Despite repeated hearings and threats she refused to recognize the authority of the court. In her biography she is recorded as saying, "I know of no offence whereof I should confess myself guilty. Having made no offence, I need no trial." Her motivation seems to have been to avoid the questioning and possible torture of her children, to give evidence against her. However, not giving a plea, guilty or not guilty, meant an automatic sentence of death. The judges and councillors all made clear the barbarity of the sentence—to be pressed to death—in an attempt to persuade her to change her mind.

Margaret was fully determined to maintain her faith as a matter of conscience and was sentenced to death under the ancient law of *peine forte et dure* ("hard and forceful punishment") on 15 March. On 25 March 1586, the Feast of the Annunciation to Mary and that year also Good Friday, Margaret was taken to the toll-booth on Ouse Bridge for execution. It is said that the four sergeants responsible were unwilling to carry out the sentence and paid four beggars to take their place. She was stripped and laid flat on the ground with a stone beneath her back. Her own door was placed on her and then weights of more than 700 pounds added. This was much heavier than was usually applied in these circumstances and she died in about fifteen minutes—in some cases it took days for the prisoner to die.

Her reasons for being prepared to die were not understood at the time; her stepfather Henry May, the Lord Mayor of York, accused her of committing suicide. Other people thought her mad. Her fellow Catholics saw her as a martyr: her silence certainly meant that other recusants were not revealed. Later they secretly retrieved her body so they could bury her with Catholic funeral rites. One hand was taken as a relic and can still be seen in the chapel of the Bar Convent in York. Margaret Clitherow was canonized in October 1970 as one of the Forty English Martyrs, one of the few women on the list.

Looking back, we are perhaps less aware of the deep fear of invasion by a mighty Spanish army and more struck by Margaret's appeal to private conscience. In itself that was a remarkable development of understanding at that time, a move away from a reliance on external authorities alone, though of course Margaret's own conviction was also based on the authority of the Pope and the Roman Catholic Church.

Though she would not have been inclined to quote scripture, in our day we might see her as a person of conscience and apply these words to her and others who find themselves pressed to deny their deepest convictions:

> Keep your conscience clear, so that, when you are maligned, those who abuse you for your good conduct in Christ may be put to shame.
>
> *1 Peter 3:16*

Mary Ward (1585–1645)

The story of Margaret Clitherow is a salutary reminder of religious persecution in the time of Elizabeth I and that period of turbulence continued for several decades. Mary Ward was a courageous successor in the Catholic faith who was fortunate not to be martyred for her faith. She inspired many other women to greater devotion to God and care for the poor.

Mary was born in 1585 near Ripon into an old Yorkshire family which had remained Roman Catholic. The following years saw the executions of Margaret Clitherow and Mary, Queen of Scots, and when Mary Ward was only three the attempted invasion by the Spanish Armada. She was brought up on stories of the faith and present-day Catholic martyrs. At the age of ten she and her sisters were caught in a fire in their house and prayed to the Blessed Virgin Mary for help; they were rescued by their father Marmaduke. As a teenager Mary heard much about convent life and by fifteen had decided that this, and not marriage, was God's call to her. She began to discipline herself, realizing that following such a call would mean leaving England. In 1606 she entered a convent of

Poor Clares (an enclosed order of nuns in the Franciscan tradition) at St
Omer, France, as a lay sister. The following year she took the remarkable
step of founding a house for Englishwomen at Gravelines. But she soon
discovered she was not called to the contemplative life, and she resolved
to devote herself to more active work amongst the poor and destitute.

By the age of twenty-four Mary found herself with a group of devoted
companions who had caught her vision of prayer, caring for the poor
and re-evangelizing England. In 1609 they established themselves as an
unofficial religious community at St Omer, and opened schools for both
wealthy and poor girls. It was a success, but it was a highly controversial
novelty, because it was set up as an unenclosed order, without religious
clothing and, like the Jesuits, not under the jurisdiction of the local
bishop. Later she was to write:

> There is no such difference between men and women, that women
> may not do great matters, as we have seen by the example of many
> Saints who have done great things; and I hope in God, it will be
> seen that women in time to come will do much.*

Borrowing so much from the Society of Jesus (itself an object of suspicion
and hostility in many quarters) and pushing the boundaries of what
women might do increased the mistrust that Mary's group inspired.
Theologians were asked for their opinions and the case eventually
went to Pope Paul V in Rome. In the late sixteenth century Pope Pius
V had declared solemn vows and strict enclosure to be essential to all
communities of religious women. This rule caused the difficulties Mary
Ward faced, even as her institute spread in Flanders, Bavaria, Austria and
Italy. She had to spend much time in Rome meeting successive popes,
seeking permission for her innovative work to be officially recognized.
She was allowed to set up a school in Rome in 1622 and then other cities,
but she remained under suspicion for many years, and was questioned
by cardinals and the Inquisition.

She did manage to travel into northern Europe in the 1620s to
strengthen the schools and houses being set up there, but she was back

---

*   Gillian Orchard (ed.), *Till God Wills* (London: DLT, 1985), p. 57.

in Rome by 1628 still trying to persuade the Pope and the authorities of her soundness and the appropriate decision to recognize her institute. The "Jesuitesses", as her congregation was designated by her opponents, were suppressed in 1630. Mary was kept under a form of house arrest and exchanged secret letters with her supporters, using lemon juice as an invisible ink!

The continued travel and the stress of seeking approval was wearing on her health, but when she received permission to travel to Germany in 1633, she did so despite being ill. Returning to Rome the following year, it was thought she might die, and this seems to have softened some attitudes to her. Eventually she was able to return to England in 1639, with a letter of introduction from Pope Urban VIII to the queen, Henrietta Maria, herself a Catholic from France. It was some thirty-three years since Mary had left England.

Mary set up her household in London, but in September 1642 she fled to the village of Hutton Rudby in the north of Yorkshire (close to the shrine of Our Lady at Mount Grace—see Day 1) to escape from the Civil War. After the battle of Marston Moor in 1644 she moved for safety into the city of York, which was besieged for six weeks by the Parliamentarians. After the siege, during which she sought to comfort people, she went with her companions to a house in Heworth, where she died soon after. Their commitment to Mary illustrates well one of her frequent sayings: "Once a friend, always a friend."

She was buried in the churchyard of Osbaldwick just outside York, a less conspicuous place, and her gravestone is now preserved inside the church. It offers an interesting summing up of her life:

> To love the poore
> persever in the same,
> live, dy and Rise with
> them was all the ayme
> of
> Mary Ward who
> Having lived 60 years
> and 8 days, dyed the
> 20 of Jan 1645.

The work of her institute continued in York for a time, and in Paris, Rome and Munich. The institute still exists, and the Bar Convent in York continues that work, having been set up in 1686 to educate girls. The most famous person to come from the Institute of the Blessed Virgin Mary is probably Mother Teresa of Calcutta, who wrote a foreword to *Till God Will*, a collection of Mary's writings.

Despite her upbringing in a time of religious turmoil and her harsh treatment by her own church when seeking for women what was possible for men in religious orders, she remained graceful to the end, devoted to God and the Virgin Mary, and working for the poor, especially girls. Her example leaves us with a challenge to care for those in need and to seek justice for others.

Joseph Rowntree (1836–1925)

Chocolate! Yes, York has been a sweet spot for chocolate and confectionery for over 200 years, and this seam in the city's history has a place in our exploration of God's people. Of the three family firms that emerged in the city to make confectionery the most pre-eminent was Rowntree, and its most significant member was Joseph. Starting work in the family grocery firm, he also helped his younger brother, who was struggling with a small cocoa business. Joseph developed this into a major firm over half a century, putting into practice good business principles and his Quaker values. By the end of his life he was known as much for his care of the people of York and his charitable work as for his successful chocolate factory.

Joseph was born at Pavement, York, one of five children of Joseph and Sarah Rowntree, who ran a grocery business. Joseph senior was also a keen educationalist, helping to found the Bootham School with his fellow Quaker, Samuel Tuke. Joseph attended this school and was also given practical lessons by his father: in 1848 he and his older brother John were taken to Ireland to see the effects of the famine there. This impressed on them the horrors of poverty and the need to find ways to alleviate it. Later Joseph was apprenticed to his father in the family business which he and John managed after their father's death in 1859.

Joseph married a fellow Quaker, Julia Eliza Seebohm, in 1856. Sadly she died in 1863, and he subsequently married her cousin, Antoinette

Seebohm, in 1867. They had four sons and two daughters in a marriage that lasted over fifty-six years.

In 1862 their younger brother, Henry Isaac, acquired the cocoa, chocolate and chicory firm of the Tukes. However, he had no head for business, and in 1869 Joseph became his partner. Much later, Joseph described his brother as financially "hopelessly embarrassed" and ignorant of the details of the cocoa trade. Henry Isaac oversaw the manufacturing, while Joseph supervised sales and bookkeeping, but it was a difficult time for them through the 1870s. In 1881 the breakthrough came not with chocolate but with fruit pastilles, which had previously been imported from France. The brothers believed in making goods of the highest quality, motivated by their Quaker ideals, and like other firms, such as Fry's and Cadbury's, found this made good business sense as well as being ethical.

When Henry Isaac died in 1883 Joseph became the sole proprietor of a firm with substantial debts which were slowly reduced. In 1887 the firm finally produced a cocoa essence called Elect, more than twenty years after Cadbury's had done something similar. Its success and the development of fruit gums led to the building of the Cocoa Works, on a twenty-nine-acre site on the edge of York. The success of the firm can be seen in the growth of its workforce, from 200 in 1883, to 894 in 1894 and 4,000 by 1906. By the beginning of the twentieth century Rowntree's had become one of the best recognized food companies in the country and, like others founded by Quakers, was trusted for high standards.

Joseph believed that wealth was to be used responsibly and he initiated a series of improvements, first for his own workers and then more widely in the city. For example, in 1891 he appointed a female welfare worker, and in 1900 a boys' welfare officer. In the next decade the firm established sick and provident funds, a doctor's surgery, a savings scheme, a school for girls, a pension scheme, a school for boys and a sick benefit scheme. These benefits were all being discussed more widely at that time, but Rowntree introduced them voluntarily before they became government policy.

Like many cities and towns in Victorian Britain, York had expanded enormously during the nineteenth century and most of the population lived in desperately poor conditions, overcrowded, and disease-ridden.

Many people died very young. In 1899 Joseph's son, Benjamin Seebohm, began a survey of all the city's working-class families. Although some improvements to living standards had been made by then he and his team discovered nearly 3,000 families living in sub-standard housing. These slums were crowded, cold and dirty, there were no proper water supplies and overflowing privies were shared by many households. The report *Poverty: A Study of Town Life* was published in 1901 and was hugely influential, as it was the first time anyone had shown the extent of poverty in a British city outside of London. His detailed and careful approach meant that he was able to use his evidence to influence social reforms introduced by the Liberal government from 1906 onwards.

Joseph acted immediately in buying land on the edge of York at New Earswick to build a model village. Houses and other facilities were built over the coming years not just for Rowntree's workers but as the trust deed put it "for the improvement of the condition of the working classes . . . by the provision of improved dwellings with open spaces and where possible gardens". To take this work forward Joseph founded a housing charity in 1904, alongside other charities for social reform, and its work can still be seen in various parts of the city in a continuing legacy.

His depth of understanding is evident in this extract from his Founder's Memorandum written in 1904:

> I feel that much of the current philanthropic effort is directed to remedying the more superficial manifestations of weakness or evil, while little thought or effort is directed to search out their underlying causes. Obvious distress or evil generally evokes so much feeling that the necessary agencies for alleviating it are pretty adequately supported.
>
> For example, it is much easier to obtain funds for the famine-stricken people in India than to originate and carry through a searching enquiry into the causes and recurrence of these famines.*

---

*   <https://archive.rowntreesociety.org.uk/
joseph-rowntrees-1904-memorandum/>.

Joseph continued as chairman of the firm in the twentieth century, gradually reducing his involvement and eventually retiring in 1923. Throughout this time, he lived a relatively modest life, preferring to support the charities he had founded and his fellow Quakers. He was a committed member of the Friargate Quaker meeting in the centre of York and attended their mostly silent worship thousands of times; he is only once recorded as having spoken in a meeting! He died at his home, Clifton Lodge, on 24 February 1925 and was buried in the Quaker cemetery at the Retreat, the hospital founded by Quakers for mentally ill people. There is no public access to this cemetery.

Although Joseph Rowntree was not particularly pioneering in his business methods or even his charitable activities (the Cadburys of Birmingham were there before him) he showed deep and lasting commitment to Christian values of care and compassion for everyone. He demonstrated honesty, integrity and humility in his business and used his wealth for the good of others. In setting out principles for the use of his money he was more supportive of education than buildings, as he believed it was easier to raise funds for buildings. Few people will have anything like the financial resources he had but, just as Mary Ward challenges us to care for the poor from few resources, we can be challenged by Rowntree to make good use of what we do have for the benefit of all. For example, it is easy to imagine Joseph and Seebohm Rowntree supporting the work of the Fair Trade movement today.

Places

Shrine of St Margaret Clitherow at 35–36 The Shambles

The Shambles in York was where the butchers lived and sold meat, and this was where Margaret joined John Clitherow when they married. It is now thought that their house was opposite the present-day shrine. The street is currently best known for its plethora of Harry Potter shops, but the shrine is part way along the street on the south side. There is an oval green plaque outside the door.

Inside is an oasis for prayer and reflection on Margaret's life and religious persecution. There is more emphasis now on finding common ground—here is a place where we can stop and pray for all who encounter religious persecution today.

Information on the shrine can be found here:

- <http://www.stwilfridsyork.org.uk/shrine-st-margaret-clitherow. php>

There is also a plaque commemorating Margaret on the Ouse Bridge, close to the place of her execution.

- <https://yorkcivictrust.co.uk/heritage/civic-trust-plaques/ st-margaret-clitherow-15523–1586/>

Bar Convent at 17 Blossom Street, York

The Bar Convent was established in 1686 by Frances Bedingfield, an early member of Mary Ward's Institute, in response to Sir Thomas Gascoigne's words, "We must have a school for our daughters." There is a beautiful chapel hidden upstairs, and you can have a guided tour. The chapel includes a priest's hole which was never used, and the relic hand of Margaret Clitherow is on display in a glass-fronted cabinet.

- <https://www.bar-convent.org.uk/>

Friargate Meeting House, Friargate, off Clifford Street, York

This is the most important Quaker building in the city, and one of the largest "meetings" in the country outside London. The present Meeting House dates from 1884 and is on the site of the first Meeting House founded in 1674. In keeping with Quaker tradition there is no memorial to Rowntree though there are books about him in the small library. Do ask for help.

There are helpful online leaflets with a Rowntree theme, covering the city centre and four other parts of the city. They indicate the massive impact the Rowntree family had on York.

- <https://www.rowntreesociety.org.uk/rowntree-now/ publications/rowntree-walks-rowntree-talks/>

Finally, as promised, there is a chocolate trail which does include some Rowntree sites:

- <https://www.visityork.org/dbimgs/Chocolate%20Map.pdf>

Prayer

God of the poor and the outcast
in the very different lives of Margaret Clitherow,
    Mary Ward and Joseph Rowntree
we see people finding ways to live out their faith
supporting minorities
searching out the poor
initiating social change.
Help us to live out our faith in practical ways
that make a difference to the most needy.

Other places

York has such a rich and long history that a whole variety of themed visits and trails has been developed. The websites listed above give information on many places linked to the saints in this book. Here are some further more general websites which provide information on other sites in the city. This can help you plan your own visit depending on your interests.

A large series of heritage trails covering many themes, including Guy Fawkes, Jewish Heritage and Saints and Sinners:

- <https://yorkcivictrust.co.uk/heritage/heritagetrails/>

Brief information on the history of the oldest church buildings in the centre of York:

- <http://secretyork.com/churches/>

Find out about some of the churches active in the city centre today. This is not a complete list!

- <https://sites.google.com/site/citycentrechurchesyork/>
- <http://www.stwilfridsyork.org.uk/>
- <http://www.centralmethodistyork.org.uk/>
- <https://yorkcitychurch.org.uk/>
- <https://www.trinitychurchyork.org.uk/>
- <http://www.yorkvineyard.com/>

Clifford's Tower

Clifford's Tower is important as the site of a notorious massacre of about 150 Jews in 1190; some committed suicide, others were murdered after surrendering.

It was also the site of the brutal execution of Robert Aske (see Day 2).

- <https://www.yorkpress.co.uk/news/17281891.york-civic-trust-plaques-robert-aske-leader-of-the-pilgrimage-of-grace-against-king-henry-viii/>

All Saints, North Street

This ancient church contained the cell of an anchoress, Emma Raughton, in the fifteenth century. Here is a link to a detailed talk about her life and times.

- <https://www.allsaints-northstreet.org.uk/SOM%20Talk%20april%2007.pdf>

DAY 5

Around Ripon: Layers of monastic heritage

As we have already seen, monasticism is a major feature of the Christian story in Yorkshire. The saints and places we will look at on Day 5 are all based on different forms of monasticism, including the early form of the seventh century, drawing on Roman and Irish traditions, the larger communities from the twelfth century onwards whose deep roots are Benedictine and representative of a more solitary approach to a disciplined life. Of course, even then most people lived out their lives with their families and neighbours, and the masters above them. Only a small number of people actually lived in monastic communities. We know these monastic lives more fully because the people involved were able to record and save their stories in ways not open to most others.

In learning of these saints we may appreciate there is much in their lives for which we can be thankful, but also be aware that they were not perfect. They were by turns quarrelsome, ambitious, awkward, inspiring, devoted and in need of forgiveness. It is in the realization of their full humanity that we may find inspiration to follow Christ, through our own imperfections.

People

Wilfrid (634–709/10)

Wilfrid is not always regarded as a godly person in our day, for he is now mostly remembered for his part in the supposed battle between a bureaucratic and remote Roman Church, and a spiritually sensitive Celtic

Church. There is a popular myth that Wilfrid massively damaged the Church at the Synod of Whitby by destroying the truer, spiritually alive faction and therefore the Church has never been the same since. This is not a fair picture either of the Synod or of Wilfrid himself, for he was a complex character, who inspired great affection in his followers, as well as opposition amongst many other people.

We know quite a lot about Wilfrid from Bede's *Ecclesiastical History*, and also from a second source which gives a different picture, written by Wilfrid's follower, Eddius Stephanus (Stephen). Stephen was a priest at Wilfrid's monastery of Ripon and wrote the *Life of Wilfrid* within six years of his death, fifteen years before Bede's work. It is full of rich detail, though Stephen is also somewhat biased in presenting Wilfrid as always right and his opponents as always wrong.

Wilfrid was born in 634, the son of an Anglo-Saxon noble, and within a year or so of Cuthbert, though he lived a quarter of a century longer. At the age of fourteen he joined the Northumbrian court of Oswy and found favour with the queen, Eanfled. However, he was keen to train as a monk and not long after that he entered the monastery on Holy Island, which was still under the leadership of Bishop Aidan. This was the year that Hilda (see Day 1) came back to Northumbria and started a community at the mouth of the River Wear. Wilfrid was quick to learn the Psalter and then the Gospels, and he was marked out as a man with a future—Bede noted his obedience and humility. However, it may be that the death of Aidan three years later unsettled him; soon afterwards he wanted to visit Rome.

The journey to Rome was a long one, involving a long wait in Canterbury on the way, until the Abbot of Wearmouth, Biscop Baducing, arrived, and the young Wilfrid could join his travelling party. Wilfrid then spent the best part of another year in Lyon, an important commercial and political centre. Archbishop Annemundus of Lyon took to Wilfrid and offered him a governorship and marriage to his niece; he was still not twenty!

In Rome he was instructed for a year by Archdeacon Boniface in Scripture and Canon law, including the correct way to calculate the date of Easter. Before leaving Rome Wilfrid had an audience with Pope

Eugene, who blessed him, and he set off with a baggage train loaded with relics, textiles, church plate and gemstones.

On the return journey he spent three crucial years once more in Lyon, where Archbishop Annemundus groomed him as a possible successor. Wilfrid received the monastic tonsure at the hand of the archbishop, the Roman tonsure rather than the Irish, of course. In Annemundus he saw how a bishop might work closely with the secular ruler (the local count was his brother), which was beginning to be the case in the Anglo-Saxon kingdoms of the time. One difference was the view that a church leader in this context was a public servant in the ancient tradition of the Roman Empire. Public magnificence was combined (generally) with private austerity. As aristocrats with means they could rebuke kings, distribute wealth and provide education.

That relationship was not necessarily straightforward: the archbishop was martyred at the instigation of a local ruler who feared the growing influence of the Church. Wilfrid was willing to die with the archbishop, but as a foreigner with connections he was spared to be sent back to his homeland. This traumatic experience seems to have reinforced Wilfrid's belief that this way of leading the Church and the continental practices of Gaul were correct, but it also implied that some of the practices he had learned on Holy Island were not.

This time away from Northumbria—a year in Canterbury, a year in Lyon, a year in Rome and a further three years in Lyon—was absolutely crucial for Wilfrid's development. These were major centres of Christianity, with excellent written records and up-to-date liturgical practices. He gained a wider perspective than many of his contemporaries who did not have the same opportunities for travel and direct contact with other forms of Christianity.

Once back in Northumbria, Wilfrid was active in promoting the reformed customs of worship that he had learned in Rome and Lyon. He was intelligent and well connected through his travels and his links to the royal family, and he became firm friends with Alchfrid, son of Oswy and Eanfled. Within a couple of years of his return Alchfrid gave Wilfrid oversight of the monastery at Ripon, evicting the founding monastic group from Melrose which had included Cuthbert. Wilfrid became the

Abbot of Ripon in 661, when he was still only twenty-seven, and he was ordained priest by Bishop Agilbert of Dorchester two years later.

Wilfrid was a key speaker at the Synod of Whitby, and though he won the arguments he did not win many friends. Bishop Colman chose to leave Lindisfarne after the Synod and a new bishop was needed; King Oswy chose Tuda, and then Chad (see Day 1). As part of a dynastic power play Oswy's son Alchfrid decided to send Wilfrid to Gaul for consecration.

But he was gone too long, for by the time Wilfrid returned Chad was well established as bishop, and Wilfrid's patron Alchfrid had rebelled against his father and had been killed. Wilfrid retired to his monastery at Ripon, until a new Archbishop of Canterbury, Theodore, moved Chad to Mercia and appointed Wilfrid as Bishop of York. Over the next ten years Wilfrid's work was highly effective and Ripon and Hexham were built up as major Christian centres.

Wilfrid's churches at Ripon and Hexham were constructed in the 660s and 670s. Apart from the cathedral church in York, built in the 620s (see Day 3), they were, so far as we know, the first stone buildings erected in Northumbria since the Roman legions left Britain in 410. For the Anglo-Saxons, used to single-storey timber and thatch houses, they must have seemed awesomely grand and permanent.

In our own day we tend to be romantic about simpler buildings, such as the first wooden churches. But there are important lessons in the transformation from wood to stone, lessons which may round out and challenge our sense of holiness:

- The solid stone is a physical reminder of the majesty of God, crucial in an age in which ordinary folk needed stability.
- We are called to belong to a spiritual temple in which Christ is the cornerstone, the foundation of our life together as a Christian community.
- The permanence of stone churches teaches us the value of a continuing community, able to represent the faithfulness of God.
- A further important aspect of a continuing community lies in its ability to promote learning, especially in valuing the word of God, recorded in handwritten Gospels of the highest quality.

Unfortunately, Wilfrid had the knack of making enemies as well as friends: caught up in Northumbrian politics he was banished from his bishopric three times, twice by King Ecgfrith and once by his successor, Aldfrith. Wilfrid also fell out with Oswy's son Ecgfrith by supporting his queen, Ethelthryth: she wished to remain a virgin and to enter a monastery. Wilfrid was motivated by religious aims, but he was also in danger of becoming a rival to the king, as his monasteries accumulated land and gifts, following the Gaulish pattern of independence from the ruler. Ironically, as a result of these banishments he became a successful missionary bishop in Frisia (Holland) and among the pagan Anglo-Saxons in Sussex and the Isle of Wight. In his late forties (681), he travelled to Sussex, which still worshipped pagan gods, and began to preach the good news of salvation. Bede recounts that the people were suffering a dreadful famine and that Wilfrid taught them how to fish in the sea. After some months of this people's hearts were opened, and many were baptized during his five-year stay.

After final, though partial, vindication by the Pope in 705 he was made Bishop of Hexham and after many years of dispute the monasteries of Ripon and Hexham were restored to him. He died in 709 at another of his monasteries at Oundle in Northamptonshire and taken back for burial at his favourite site of Ripon.

Wilfrid's example of holiness is difficult to accept today and was controversial even in his own time. But he clearly did have loyal followers, who recognized his personal commitment to Christ, and who knew that his own lifestyle was austere. This often makes people uncomfortable because he was also committed to seeking power and influence for the Church. Wilfrid's life poses difficult questions about whether holiness should only be a matter of private lifestyle, or whether and how it should also include the ways we organize our society.

Thurstan of York (about 1070–1140)

A collection of God's Own People in Yorkshire which didn't include an Archbishop of York would seem odd, but who to choose? Remember, the seventh-century characters already mentioned—Paulinus, John of Beverley, Chad and Wilfrid—were all Bishops of York, but they were not archbishops, a title which was first used in 735. Among the nearly one hundred holders of the office there are real saints and some eccentrics (a relatively polite term when one—Lancelot Blackburne in the eighteenth century—is said to have begun his career as a pirate!). I have chosen Thurstan as someone whose life exemplified both the ambiguity of holding spiritual and political power at the same time, with a desire to see spiritual transformation. His story provides an interesting "compare and contrast" with that of Wilfrid.

Thurstan was born into a clerical family in Normandy just after the Norman Conquest of England. His father was a priest and his brother Audoin also followed suit, later becoming a bishop. Thurstan was educated in Normandy, but his family moved to London when he was a young man as part of the wider movement of Normans into positions of influence in English society. The brothers became chaplains under King Henry I, positions which were as much about royal administration as religious duties. We know almost nothing about Thurstan's specific activities on behalf of the king, but Henry's decision to make him an archbishop shows how much he must have been valued. In his younger days Thurstan visited the monastery at Cluny and made a vow to take on the monastic habit at some point in his life.

Thurstan comes to our notice in 1114 when Henry I appointed him as Archbishop of York, without any reference to the chapter of clergy there. Fortunately they raised no objections and by the end of the year he had been ordained as a deacon. However, his path to becoming archbishop and active in his diocese was tortuous and lengthy, involving much travelling and many arguments over the next seven years. At the heart of the disputes was a question of status and authority: did the Archbishop of York have to swear obedience to the Archbishop of Canterbury or not? Getting an answer involved the King of England, two archbishops and no less than three popes. In 1118–19 the third of these popes, Calixtus II, ruled in favour of York and, against Henry's wishes at the time, consecrated Thurstan as archbishop at Rheims in northern France.

Henry refused to accept what had happened at first, but through a series of diplomatic meetings, including one between the king and the Pope, they began to find a way forward. Thurstan was kept in France and became useful in negotiations between Henry and the King of France. He also met with Henry's sister, Adele, and was a spiritual mentor to her.

Much later when back in England, Thurstan was to take the side of her son, Stephen, in the civil war between him and Henry's daughter, Matilda, that began in 1135.

By 1121, under pressure from the Pope, Henry I allowed Thurstan to return to England and to take up the archbishopric of York. There was plenty to occupy him: early on he attempted, with the Pope's agreement, to obtain the obedience of the bishops in Scotland. In this he was not successful, but he was involved in diplomatic discussions with the Scottish King David as well as the bishops. To enhance the reputation of his archbishopric he was able to create two new posts for bishops in Galloway and in Carlisle. The creation of a diocese based on Carlisle was also a political decision involving King Henry and it demonstrates how Thurstan was able to combine spiritual and political realities, re-establishing a long-standing relationship with the king.

Thurstan is also remembered for his support of monastic life across his large diocese. He founded a small hospital in Ripon and two monasteries, the first of which was a small nunnery called St Clement's in York. This was the first women's religious community formed north of the River Trent after the Norman Conquest of 1066, and led to an upsurge of such houses across the north of England. His second foundation is now much better known but came about almost accidentally. In 1132 a group of Cistercian monks passed through York on their way to the new foundation at Rievaulx. While staying at St Mary's Abbey in York an argument broke out over how best to live out their monastic vows. As a result Thurstan was called in to adjudicate. He appears to have sided with the stricter Cistercian party, for when thirteen monks were expelled from St Mary's they joined the archbishop's household on a temporary basis. They joined him for Christmas at Ripon and soon after he gave them land by the River Skell to form a new house, which we now know as Fountains Abbey. The grand buildings whose ruins we see took centuries to build and the first few years there were very precarious for the monks there.

Thurstan's support for the monastic life probably played a part in Aelred's call to Rievaulx (see Day 1) and in creating a monastic site at Byland. Beyond that he also encouraged Augustinian foundations at Nostell, Guisborough, Kirkham, Bolton, Drax and Worksop. The

Augustinian canons of these places also acted as parish priests and thus enabled Thurstan to improve the pastoral care in his diocese.

In 1137, towards the end of his life, Thurstan was again involved in diplomatic negotiations with King David of Scotland. The truce broke down a year later and on behalf of King Stephen Thurstan called together a northern army which fought against the Scots near Northallerton. It became known as the Battle of the Standard, after the standard Thurstan made from the banners of St Peter of York, St John of Beverley and St Wilfrid of Ripon. He was too ill to attend the subsequent peace conference and, shortly before his death in February 1140, Thurstan took the monastic habit at the Cluniac priory of Pontefract. He was buried there in front of the high altar.

As we saw in the life of Wilfrid, holding high office in the Church has often involved great opportunities for good alongside very real temptations to pride and the abuse of power. However, both men were admired for their devotion to following Christ and personal examples of generosity and self-discipline. An early biographer of Thurstan also praised his steadfastness, his sense of principle, his devotion to the cause of religious women and pastoral care. He was able to gain and keep the affection and respect of the king whom he had opposed, and he did much to strengthen the Church in his vast diocese.

Robert Flower of Knaresborough (died 1218)

Like another character we will encounter (Richard Rolle, Day 7), Robert Flower was a hermit. There were at least fourteen hermitages in Yorkshire in the twelfth century. To us a hermit conjures up an image of someone living far away from other people, having very little contact with the rest of society. In practice, hermits mostly lived alone but had considerable interaction with other people and were often important in the development of local communities. That was certainly the case with Robert Flower and Richard Rolle.

Robert Flower was prepared to challenge the religious and political establishments of his day. He set up what we would now call a food bank and people believed he had the power of miraculous healing. Until recently he has been a neglected figure, but his memory and legacy have been revived in Knaresborough, and he deserves a wider audience.

Robert came from a prosperous and pious family in York. His parents, Took and Siminima Flower, took his education very seriously, especially concentrating on his spiritual and moral development. As a young man he spent time in the churches and monasteries of York, and he considered becoming a priest. For some unknown reason this never happened but he did go away to a small monastery called Newminster, near Morpeth. This developed his spiritual life, but he stayed there only four months as he believed that God was calling him elsewhere.

He joined a hermit in Knaresborough but it was not long before his fellow hermit, who was a knight, returned to his wife and children, leaving Robert without any means to sustain himself. Fortunately a devout widow stepped in, and he was given the chapel of St Hilda the Virgin at Rudfarlington, south of Knaresborough. (The site is now occupied by a farm.) He stayed there for a year, living off the land on his own, and using the opportunity for contemplation and self-denial. He also collected food for the poor, which unfortunately was stolen when thieves broke in.

Robert decided to leave for the nearby village of Spofforth in order to continue his prayer life. This time he attracted the unwanted attention of the local people to such an extent that he had to move on once again. He found sanctuary with a small community of monks living at Hedley, a few miles from Tadcaster. However, he seemed determined to live even more austerely than his hosts: according to his biographer, he wore just a thin white habit, made bread from four parts wheat and a fifth part sieved ashes, and refused to eat any meat. Not surprisingly, he became unpopular with his community and he soon returned to the chapel of St Hilda at Rudfarlington.

This time he formed a small community of his own, in which he could set the rule for living. He continued to spend long periods in prayer at night, while during the day he and his community farmed the land and collected money for the poor and needy. This care for the poor came to the attention of the local lord, Sir William Stuteville. He took a violent dislike to Robert's work, claiming "This man is an abettor and harbourer of thieves and robbers." He provoked the local people to tear down Robert's buildings, so that Robert moved on once more.

In this final move he went back to Knaresborough and the chapel of St Giles where he had stayed before. Living in a simple shelter he continued his contemplative life, attracting a stream of visitors who wanted to deepen their faith by spending time with him. According to his earliest biographer his focus at this time was on the spiritual needs of his hearers, and he supplied food only to the very poorest pilgrims.

His brother Walter, who was Mayor of York, visited Robert and wanted to provide him with better accommodation. Unsurprisingly, Robert resisted this, but he did accept help in developing the little chapel and hermitage by the River Nidd which can still be seen today. After so much travel in his life this became Robert's final home and he continued to support the poor and to challenge the wealthy and powerful.

Among many stories told about him perhaps the most significant is of his encounter with King John, who visited Knaresborough Castle in 1216. The new lord, Sir Brian de l'Isle, persuaded the king to visit Robert's hermitage. Robert was prostrate in prayer and did not rise for the king until urged by Sir Brian. In response to this rebuke Robert picked up an ear of corn and asked the king, "Is your power such, my lord king, that you can make something like this out of nothing?" The people listening to the conversation were split between those who saw this as great stupidity and those who saw it as godly wisdom. The king gave Robert land to cultivate in order to provide for the poor: it would seem that Robert was right to be bold in the presence of King John, despite his fearsome reputation.

At the end of Robert's life in 1218 there was a dispute over where he would be buried, so heated that it required the intervention of an armed force from Knaresborough Castle. His reputation was such that the monks of Fountains Abbey wanted him as a draw for pilgrims, having no great saint of their own. In the end Robert's wish to be buried in his cell was respected and it became a place where many people came to seek healing. Today the site has been made accessible by a wooden staircase and there is a wooden statue which commemorates the 800th anniversary of his death.

Robert Flower comes across as a somewhat driven character. He took his devotion to God seriously and tried to care for the poor and disadvantaged around him. At the same time he also seems to have quite deliberately looked to confront other people, whether local landowners, fellow monks or even the king. Ultimately the balance seems to be that his actions speak of love for those around him, collecting food and alms for the poor, being ready with a thoughtful word or prayer for healing, and standing up against injustice when he could.

His legacy is summed up by the two references next to his new statue. The first is: "Becoming like Christ, serving others." The second is from Luke 10:27: "You shall love the Lord your God with all your heart, and with all your soul, and with all your strength, and with all your mind; and your neighbour as yourself."

I am grateful not to have to live in a cave next to a river, but I have to recognize that the challenge to love and serve God and my neighbour is just as real for me as it was for Robert of Knaresborough.

Places

Ripon

Ripon is another of Yorkshire's lovely market towns. It has a long history and some special traditions including that of the horn blower who plays around 9pm every evening in the town's beautiful square, to "set the watch". Naturally this visit concentrates on Ripon Cathedral, which dominates the town and is a short walk from the square. This is the fourth church on the site, and it was begun in the twelfth century to encourage pilgrimage to the tomb of Wilfrid. In 1836 it became the cathedral of the new diocese of Ripon, and in 2014 one of the cathedrals of the diocese of Leeds.

You enter via a modern glass screen with beautiful etchings, which are perhaps best seen looking from the inside out. It is a welcoming space and entry is free. As you take time to absorb the peaceful atmosphere go forward to the screen in front of the choir. The painted statues include Thurstan on the left-hand side, along with other kings, bishops, and saints associated with the cathedral's long history.

The highlight of the tour is the crypt which dates back to Wilfrid himself: it is the only part of the fabric which remains from his time here. Entry is down a steep, narrow staircase, modelled on the shrines of saints that Wilfrid had seen in Rome. It is a very small shrine inside but was the focus of visits for hundreds of years. According to the present dean (John

Dobson) it is the oldest piece of cathedral fabric in Britain. He also judges it to be the oldest place of continuous prayer in England. It is certainly a good place to pause and thank God for all those who have lived out and passed on the Christian faith through nearly fourteen centuries.

Ripon is connected to our next destination by a special pilgrim route which roughly follows the route taken by Thurstan's thirteen monks in the winter of 1132–33. It goes from the city along the River Skell, through Studley Royal Deer Park and on to the National Trust site at Fountains Abbey. The route is taken by hundreds of pilgrims on Boxing Day each year after a short service in the cathedral—check the website for details.

- <http://www.riponcathedral.org.uk/>

Fountains Abbey

Fountains Abbey today is an archetypal picturesque site; its substantial ruins are well maintained by the National Trust, with easy access and excellent interpretation. Its humble origins in 1132 have been overlaid by four centuries of monastic building and its incorporation into the pleasure gardens of Studley Royal in the eighteenth century. Walking from one of the car parks to the ruins is straightforward; imagining how it might have been in the twelfth century for the first monks requires some effort. The valley of the River Skell remains enclosed, but the river channel has been tamed and beautified. There are woods and footpaths to follow so, if you can, do try to get off the beaten track and ponder the lives of those first monks.

The impressive ruins we see today represent the last stages of the monastery's life, including a final flourishing in the early sixteenth century, just before the dissolution of the monasteries under Henry VIII. They are claimed to be the largest monastic ruins in England. However, despite what became extensive land holdings and a sometimes profitable business in wool from Dales sheep, it had quite a troubled history. Early on many of the buildings were burnt down by a mob which was angry with the then abbot for opposing a candidate for the archbishopric of York, and later the community suffered from poor management of its woollen business. Invasions by Scots armies and finally the Black Death of the mid-fourteenth century all added to its troubles. But the monks also gained a good reputation for caring for the poor and sick in the area, and providing food in times of famine whenever they could.

There is an excellent exhibition and models of the abbey in the Porter's Lodge, just to the west of the present ruins. The history is well laid out and explained in the former gatehouse, which now offers access to understanding the abbey's story. Once you've learned more of this, take time to wander round the ruins and consider the lives of the monks and the many lay brothers who did much of the hard physical work. Even when there are many visitors it is usually possible to find a quiet spot for reflection and prayer.

- <https://www.nationaltrust.org.uk/ fountains-abbey-and-studley-royal-water-garden/the-abbey>

Knaresborough

The best place to get a flavour of Robert Flower of Knaresborough's life is at the remains of his cave and chapel by the River Nidd on the outskirts of the town. The north bank of the river is tree-lined along this section and you need to look out for a small parking place and a new information board. Walking down the steep wooden staircase you have a striking wooden statue of Robert before you. For me, it represents Robert in his later years, as a man who has found peace and wants to share that with others. This is where you can find the plaque with the inscription "Becoming like Christ, serving others" and Luke 10:27.

Although about 500 hermitages are mentioned in documents from the Middles Ages, only a few survive today. This is an especially good example to visit because it is possible to see the foundations of the chapel and evidence of the living space, mainly in a cave cut into the rock. The cave is large enough to go inside and explore, especially with a torch. It is a quiet spot in which you can take time to reflect on Robert's life and your own. Within the remains of the chapel the place where Robert was buried is still marked, though his body was long ago moved to a priory in Knaresborough.

Other sites nearby have some association with Robert: the castle from where the local lords ruled over the district is a spectacular ruin. A little further away at Rudfarlington is an old farm on the site of the chapel of St

Hilda that Robert occupied. Sadly no traces remain. Another four miles west, in the village of Pannal, you can visit the only Church of England building dedicated to St Robert. There are no specific memorials to him but information in leaflets and booklets is available.

- <https://www.strobertsharrogate.co.uk/ st-robert-of-knaresborough-800th-anniversary/>

Prayer

Gracious God, you call us all to lives of devotion.
We give thanks for those people who lived
    this call through a monastic life.
Help us as we seek space devoted to you
conscious of your presence around and within us
aware of your work in other people
sensitive to your whole creation.
Through Christ who devoted his life for others.

Practicalities

Ripon
Ripon is easily reached by car from the A1 and has the facilities of a small town with attractive shops and accommodation. Driving to Fountains Abbey is very straightforward if you are not taking the walking option. Buses run from Harrogate, but there is no longer a train station.

Knaresborough
Knaresborough is easily reached by car from the A1, and buses run from various locations too. Both Knaresborough and Pannal are on the train line between York and Harrogate.

The remains of Robert of Knaresborough's cave and chapel are on the southern edge of the town by the River Nidd.

There is a pleasant 7½-mile pilgrimage walk linking Pannal Church, the farm at Rudfarlington and ending at the cave by the River Nidd:

- <http://strobertofknaresborough.org.uk/wp-content/uploads/2018/09/St-Roberts-Way_1.pdf>

Other places

Yorkshire is rich in abbeys, and here are three more evocative sites not too far from today's. They were all involved in the 1536 Pilgrimage of Grace (see Day 2), and each was dissolved soon after the rebellion was suppressed.

Jervaulx Abbey

Jervaulx Abbey was another Cistercian abbey, founded in 1152 in lower Wensleydale. Its final abbot was Adam Sedbergh, who was caught up in the Pilgrimage of Grace and was executed by being hanged, drawn and quartered at Tyburn in 1537. The site is now privately owned but it is open to visitors during daylight hours and operates an honesty box. Refreshments are available on site.

- <https://www.jervaulxabbey.com/>

Coverham Abbey

A little further up Wensleydale are the remains of Coverham Abbey, founded here in 1212. There is not a great deal to see here, but it can be glimpsed from the redundant parish church. It is worth checking for any special events which are held from time to time.

- <https://www.britainexpress.com/attractions.htm?attraction=2733>

Easby Abbey

Easby Abbey is just downstream on the River Swale from the delightful town of Richmond.

It was founded in the late twelfth century, by Premonstratensian "White Canons", with a layout very similar to those of the Cistercian order. It was dissolved in 1536 as a result of its involvement in the Pilgrimage of Grace. There are still substantial atmospheric ruins to wander round. If you have been to other sites in the area you will notice how the usual monastic layout has been constrained by its location close to the River Swale.

- <https://www.english-heritage.org.uk/visit/places/easby-abbey>

In the West Riding: Coping with industrialization

During the Middle Ages the West Riding tended to be less prosperous than the North and East Ridings, and so there are fewer large churches from that period than in other parts of the county. As industry developed so the population grew, and as the Industrial Revolution took hold from the mid-eighteenth century, cities and towns expanded rapidly. In that context many Christian ministers saw a need to express the good news in ways that made sense in these new urban settings. The characters I have chosen for this day are significant in their own right but also represent many other people whose names are less well known. We begin with Henry Venn at the beginning of this period, bridging the gap between rural and urban as Huddersfield expanded. A generation later came Richard Oastler, a businessman who, because of his faith, became an agitator for the reform of working conditions, especially for children. Our third character, Smith Wigglesworth, was a working man who became a preacher, evangelist and faith healer together with his wife, Polly. They shared their faith from a position of equality and Smith was known as the "plumber-preacher".

Today's places may not be obvious sites for pilgrimage but learning a little more about the people who lived and worked here may open our eyes to the ways God can be at work in present-day cities.

People

Henry Venn (1725–97)

The saints of Yorkshire include people who were not born in the county and did not live in it for very long, but whose lives of dedication and commitment made a big impact on those around them. Henry Venn was the vicar of Huddersfield for twelve years in the eighteenth century and gave spiritual support to many hundreds of people, rich and poor, influential and apparently insignificant. Even half a century after he had left Huddersfield he was still remembered with deep affection.

Henry was born in Surrey into a family of clergymen, as far back as the Reformation. His father, Richard, was a very respectable and conventional vicar who was the first minister in London to forbid the evangelical George Whitefield to preach in his parish. Henry was later to work closely with Whitefield! After a private education he went to Cambridge University in 1742, gaining his degree in 1745 and continuing his studies there. He was a great cricketer, but just before his ordination in 1747 he gave his bat away, saying: "I will never have it said of me 'Well struck, parson.'" It sounds a little pompous but he was also said to be friendly and a great storyteller.

After a period of further study and helping in local parishes he went to be the curate at 1749, having been elected to a fellowship at Queens' College on 30 March of that year. He also began his ministerial career in 1749, and for a short time combined his college duties with officiating at Barton, Cambridgeshire, Wadenhoe, Northamptonshire, Little Hedingham, Essex, and other local places. He ceased to reside at Cambridge in 1750 and went as curate to Adam Langley, who held the livings of St Matthew, Friday Street, London for part of the summer, and West Horsley, Surrey for the rest of the year. At West Horsley, Venn's family prayers were attended by about forty poor neighbours, and attendance at communion rose from twelve to sixty. The local clergy were less positive, believing him to be an enthusiast and Methodist, but he continued to hold the strong high-church beliefs of his father. At the same time his ministry there gave him time for reading, including William Law's *A Serious Call to a Devout and Holy Life*, a book which had had a profound influence on John Wesley. Finding it difficult to put into practice its high standards, he seems to have found help in John Wesley's writings and the idea of justification by faith. He wrote to Wesley saying that his writings "be as thunder to my drowsy soul". From this point in 1754 all his preaching and teaching came from this evangelical perspective.

That same year Venn became curate of Clapham, an affluent village south of London, which was becoming a centre of the evangelical revival. He also lectured at two London churches and had to preach so many sermons that he had to speak extempore or from short notes, which he continued to do for the rest of his life. At Clapham Venn was soon connected with many leaders of evangelical Christianity, including Wesley, Whitefield and the very wealthy businessman John Thornton, whose family originally came from Hull.

During a severe illness in 1756 he had even more time for self-examination and reflection. He began to write a devotional book, *The Complete Duty of Man*, which was published in 1763. It became very popular, and over the next fifty years it was reprinted twenty times.

Venn recovered and in May 1757 he married Eling Bishop, herself a vicar's daughter. She had come to share the same beliefs as Henry and their marriage seems to have been a very happy one. They went on to have four daughters and one son, John, who himself was later ordained and became rector of Clapham. For the next two years Venn was involved in preaching tours in the West Country and in London. In his own parish the people were less receptive: many found his preaching and boldness very offensive and complained to his wife. One lady described him as a good man but complained that he alarmed people with his preaching. This was not a good idea, she told his wife, given that the family was financially dependent on the congregation. Eling replied robustly: "The Master Mr Venn serves is too great and too good ever to see him, or his, real losers for faithfulness in his own service."

This was an unhappy situation for them, and Henry later wrote that he was "grieved at the obstinate rejection of the gospel during five years by almost all the rich (and there were but few poor in the place)". In 1759 he was appointed as vicar of Huddersfield through the kindness of friends. Huddersfield was in the early stages of the expansion of the textile industry. The parish covered a wide area with about 5,000 people in the town and in outlying hamlets and farms. John Wesley had visited in October 1757 and wrote, "A wilder people I never saw in England."

Venn won people over with his preaching, praying and visiting, and by welcoming enquirers in his vicarage. On Sundays at Huddersfield large crowds soon filled the church to hear his sermons. He wanted to encourage them as worshippers and communicants and help them to understand the Prayer Book. Somewhat unusually for the time, he gave courses of preparation before Holy Communion, taught the younger members of the congregation and introduced hymn-singing into the service when most in the Church of England were said. During the week he taught throughout the parish, preaching in the open air and holding services in houses in the surrounding hamlets. On top of this he was still being asked to preach in other places in England and South Wales.

The growth in the church through his ministry led many leaders of the evangelical movement to visit Huddersfield, the first large parish held by an evangelical minister in England. This kept him in touch with colleagues across the country and he began to be seen as an inspirational figure. Unfortunately, he and John Wesley fell out over their respective understandings of salvation and Venn was dissatisfied with Methodism for the rest of his life.

His time in Huddersfield was very demanding. Besides his regular parish duties, he became a mentor to many who wanted to take their faith seriously. Although he received a stipend of £100 a year, he had considerable financial pressure: besides the care for his family he was called upon to travel extensively and to entertain many visitors. He was also very generous: his wife would make him empty his pockets before visiting people in the parish as he was inclined to give everything away! He gave his successor a register of names, indicating the "poor" and the "very poor": from the poor he took nothing and to the very poor he gave something.

The death of his wife Eling in 1767 after a long illness was very distressing and left him with five young children to care for. He was becoming exhausted and began to show signs of consumption (tuberculosis). He was able to preach only once a fortnight. In 1771 he reluctantly accepted the move to the village of Yelling, Huntingdonshire, saying, "Nothing would have prevailed upon me to leave Huddersfield if my lungs had not received an irreparable injury".

In the same year Venn married a widow, Catherine Smith, and they moved to Yelling together. As his health recovered, he built up the congregation and began to preach for a few weeks in London each year. Being close to Cambridge he was visited by students and younger clergy, most significantly Charles Simeon, who went on to become one of the great preachers of the nineteenth century. After a full twenty years at Yelling, Venn's health collapsed. In the autumn of 1791, he took on a permanent curate for the parish and after that rarely preached or led worship, though he continued his conversation and writing. He finally left Yelling in early 1797 and went to Clapham, where his son John was now rector. He died there on 24 June 1797 and was buried in the old churchyard.

Although Henry Venn was very self-disciplined, he was also remembered as a friendly and happy man and he seems to have been good company, warm and supportive in his spiritual advice. He was a lively and effective preacher who knew how to engage his hearers. One of his Huddersfield congregation explained, "When he got warm with his subject, he looked as if he would jump out of his pulpit. He made many weep." In reflecting on his life perhaps we can learn from his readiness to encourage others and his willingness to see them develop even further than he had. Later a plaque in his honour was erected in the parish church in Huddersfield, "Finding his memory still embalmed in the hearts of many at Huddersfield".

Richard Oastler (1789–1861)

Henry Venn had seen the early stages of the Industrial Revolution in Yorkshire. In succeeding decades factories sprang up all over the West Riding, drawing in workers from the countryside in search of a better living. It is sobering to realize that conditions on the land for so many people were even worse than those in the factories. For as the factory system developed the appalling working and living conditions of its workers led many people to look for reform and improvements. Among them was Richard Oastler, no longer a well-known name, but prominent in his time and compared by some with William Wilberforce (see Day

2) for his importance in challenging negative attitudes and exploitative practices.

Richard Oastler was born in 1789 in St Peter's Square, Leeds, the eighth and last child of Robert and Sarah Oastler. His father had embraced Methodism at the age of sixteen and left his family to go to Thirsk. He happened to meet John Wesley in 1766, and a friendship developed. Over time Robert became a leader in the Methodist community, and Wesley is said to have blessed Richard as a baby during his last visit in 1790.

From the age of nine Oastler attended a Moravian boarding school at Fulneck, near Leeds, where he deepened his Christian faith. When he left at the age of seventeen, he intended to become a barrister, but his father did not approve and for a time he worked with an architect. However, his eyesight was not good enough, and he became a middleman between wholesalers in Leeds and small shopkeepers across the West Riding. Soon he was "respected for his sterling integrity and honour and considered as one whose superior talents for business would shortly raise him to affluence and distinction", according to a later biographer. In 1816 Oastler married Mary Tatham, from another Wesleyan family. They had two children, Sarah and Robert. Sadly both died when infants in 1819.

Further troubles followed in 1820: his business failed and in February he was declared bankrupt. Then his father died in July 1820. As a result, he was able to succeed his father as steward to Thomas Thornhill, the absentee squire of Fixby, just north of Huddersfield. This was a complete change of life from an urban, commercial and Methodist perspective to a rural, landed and Anglican one. He took up traditional rural customs and turned against trade and industry, perhaps in a reaction to the multiple bereavements he and Mary had suffered. Nonetheless, despite nostalgic leanings he was still no social conservative.

At some point Oastler became well known as an abolitionist, supporting Wilberforce's campaign against slavery. However, he knew nothing, he later claimed, of the cruelties in English textile mills when he rode over to Bradford in September 1830 to visit his friend John Wood. According to the story of "Oastler's awakening", Wood told Oastler about the appalling conditions in the Bradford mills. Oastler immediately wrote the letter to the *Leeds Mercury* on "Yorkshire slavery" that started the factory movement. Although the story is oversimplified his letter did have a powerful impact. In it he claimed:

> thousands of our fellow creatures and fellow subjects, both male and female, the miserable inhabitants of a *Yorkshire town* . . . are this very moment existing in a state of slavery *more horrid* than are the victims of that hellish system—*"colonial slavery"* . . . thousands of little children, both male and female, but principally female, from seven to fourteen years of age, are daily compelled to labour from six in the morning to seven in the evening . . . with only thirty-minutes allowed for eating and recreation.*

Connecting factory reform with the campaign against slavery energized people across the country. In February 1831, John Cam Hobhouse, the radical MP for Westminster, proposed a Bill providing for an eleven-and-a-half-hour day for all textile workers under the age of eighteen. Fighting opposition from mill owners, Hobhouse agreed to limit its provisions to cotton mills. In response Oastler wrote an angry manifesto "to the Working Classes of the West Riding", urging workers to take up the issue. Many short-time committees were formed across Yorkshire, on the pattern of Wesleyan "class meetings", seeking a universal ten-hour day. In the Fixby Hall Compact of June 1831, Oastler and the workers of Huddersfield agreed to work together for the ten-hour day, regardless of party or sect. Though in many ways a paternalistic Tory, Oastler was also a rebel and a radical and in this cause he had found his true calling.

He testified before a parliamentary committee of enquiry and organized marches and meetings where he spoke plainly and rapidly. He was a tall and broad-shouldered man with an uncomplicated view of the world, formed by his upbringing in Methodism. His ability to speak to the crowds led to his nickname of the "Factory King".

After the general election of 1832 (following the passage of the Great Reform Act) Anthony Ashley Cooper, later 7th Earl of Shaftesbury, took up the cause of the ten-hour working day. The battle between reformers

---

* Rosemary J. Mundhenk, Luann McCracken Fletcher (eds), *Victorian Prose: An Anthology* (New York: Columbia University Press, 1999), p. 10.

and factory owners led to a series of unsatisfactory reforms and confusion in the factory movement. Oastler himself was unhappy with strikes and trade unions and even universal suffrage. However, he was strongly against the new workhouse test in the new Poor Law, believing that caring for the poor was a religious obligation, and he resisted as unchristian the 1834 Poor Law, which set up tough workhouses for the poorest in society.

Proposed changes in government policy to factory reform led Oastler to suggest he would teach children how to sabotage factory machines if the law was not applied. Up to this point his employer, Thomas Thornhill, had accepted his various campaigns but Oastler's advocacy of violence and against the new Poor Law turned Thornhill against him. He was dismissed in 1838, and Thornhill started legal proceedings against him for debt. Oastler could not pay and spent three-and-a-half years in the Fleet Prison in London.

While in prison Oastler wrote a weekly newspaper, the *Fleet Papers*, attacking the Whig government and the Poor Law, and including accounts of his own troubles. This did little to help his cause, and it was only through the efforts of friends and admirers that he was freed in February 1844. His wife died in 1845 and he retired to Guildford with the support of friends. He lived quietly and died in Harrogate in 1861. At his own request he was buried at St Stephen's Church, Kirkstall, near Leeds.

The 1847 Ten Hour Act was extended after his death to children working in all factories, not just the cotton mills. His campaigning had finally borne fruit, and the movement he had done much to energize went on to secure further reforms of the factory system. His fame was such that money was raised nationally for a memorial, and his statue was unveiled by Lord Shaftesbury in front of a crowd of over 100,000 people. It is now in Northgate Square, next to the Oastler Shopping Centre in Bradford.

Polly Wigglesworth (1850–1913) and Smith Wigglesworth (1859–1947)
The industrialization of the West Riding continued through the nineteenth century, and gradually improvements were made to living conditions for working families, and the massively expanded towns and cities acquired new infrastructure including paved streets, better access to water, public buildings and the growth of education. This was the world in which Polly Featherstone and Smith Wigglesworth grew up and pursued

a remarkable ministry. Unlike many of the characters in this book they did not come from a wealthy or influential background, and it is good to include them as an example of the variety and diversity of God's people. Smith was trained and worked as a plumber, and alongside that, with no formal training, became a preacher, evangelist and faith healer who travelled the world from his home in Bradford.

Polly was born in Scarborough, but moved with her family to Bradford and was involved with the Salvation Army from its early days. Smith was born into a family of farm labourers in the village of Menston, a few miles north of Bradford. They were poor despite being hard-working, and Smith did not learn to read and write until Polly taught him. Through attending the Wesleyan chapel with his grandmother, Smith came to a deep personal faith in Christ at the age of eight. He immediately began to share his faith, initially with his mother. He and his brother James also sang in the local parish choir, and he was confirmed at the age of twelve. In later life he recalled the experience: "My whole body was filled with the consciousness of God's presence, a consciousness that remained with me for days."

When the family moved to Bradford to work in the textile mills, he attended the local Methodist church and the Salvation Army. He also attended the early morning Holy Communion service in his parish church, St Luke's. An openness to Christians of different traditions stayed with him throughout his life. Smith had decided to be a plumber and spent three years in Liverpool learning more about this trade. While there he shared his faith—and food—with slum children, again linking up with the Salvation Army. Returning to Bradford aged twenty-three to set up his own plumbing business, he met Polly through the Salvation Army, and they were soon married and went on to have five children. The family was supported by Smith's successful business, and he became a master plumber.

They began married life round the corner from Smith's family, in 70 Victor Road, an address Smith would later play on, finding the number 70 and the concepts of victor and victory in many places in the Bible. This was their home for the rest of their lives, and it became a well-known address as a place for hospitality and prayer, and where letters would arrive with prayer requests from all over the world. Visitors would be dissuaded from reading the newspaper and instead were asked to focus on prayer and reading the Bible together: many people testified as to how helpful this was to them in drawing closer to God. "Something good happened to me in that place. I'll come back again."

Polly and Smith had the happy knack of relating well to people, even strangers. They would visit Lister Park at the bottom of the road and sit and wait for others to join them. Friendly conversations followed which frequently led to spiritual concerns and often prayer for them. In this way many people made commitments to follow Christ for themselves. Their concern for the spiritual well-being of the people of Braford led them to rent a room where they could hold meetings to encourage others to grow in faith. Smith encountered other preachers in Leeds who prayed for healing and he discovered that God used him in this way too. This work grew, and the Wigglesworths moved into a larger hall in Bowland Street, Bradford. Both Polly and Smith saw people come to faith in Christ and this remained their spiritual home for many years.

There was a further development in Smith's own spiritual life in 1907 when he learned of Pentecostal revival in an Anglican church in Sunderland. He met with the vicar, Alexander Boddy, and his wife Mary to learn more, and he received the gift of speaking in tongues (sometimes described as a prayer language not known to the speaker) after Mary laid hands on him and prayed for this gift. A lifelong friendship developed between them and Boddy frequently included items about Wigglesworth in his Pentecostal newspaper, *Confidence*. The publicity that this generated led to many more visitors to the Bowland Street Mission and invitations for Smith and Polly to speak elsewhere. This was a key friendship on both sides which survived despite some different understandings regarding the Church. (Alexander and Mary Boddy are included in my book *Holy Places, Holy People*, Day 3.)

Polly died on New Year's Day 1913 after preaching at the Bowland Street Mission. Smith had been on his way to Glasgow but was called back. In desperation, standing at her side he prayed for death to give her up and, however it happened, he had a brief conversation with her which brought him some comfort.

Though Smith missed Polly very much he continued and even expanded his preaching and healing ministry, travelling over the next three decades to the USA many times, to several European countries, to Australia and New Zealand, Sri Lanka and India, and South Africa. Despite illnesses for which he refused medical attention he was very energetic and well received in churches of many different persuasions. He wrote very little, but others took note of his sermons and he became known as the Apostle of Faith. He regularly told his congregations:

> Fear looks; faith jumps. Faith never fails to obtain its object. If I leave you as I found you, I am not God's channel. I am not here to entertain you, but to get you to the place where you can laugh at the impossible.

Smith died in 1947, having travelled to Wakefield for the funeral of a very close friend. His own funeral was held in the Elim Church, Bradford, and he was buried with Polly at the Nab Wood Cemetery north of the city. He remains an inspiring if sometimes controversial figure, but he showed how it is possible for a committed person to influence others, when he lived by what he preached and was ready to admit his own shortcomings alongside the greatness of God. For me, Polly and Smith challenge us to live with integrity and utter commitment.

Places

Huddersfield

Huddersfield is a typically rugged Pennine town, with many buildings constructed from the local millstone grit, golden when first cut but blackened over time by pollution. I have known Huddersfield for many decades as the hometown of my wife's family. It was made relatively prosperous by the growth of the textile industry from the late eighteenth century onwards, but subsequently suffered as the industry developed elsewhere in the world. Today it is seeking a new future by diversifying its industries and developing as a centre for learning—the University of Huddersfield even has its own new Oastler Building.

Huddersfield Parish Church is in the heart of the modern shopping centre and can easily be reached from the bus and railway stations.

It is an imposing building, though now slightly hemmed in by the newer buildings around it. The present church was built just before the Reformation in 1503–6 and was significantly rebuilt in the 1830s as the town had grown so much. There are references to Henry Venn in the list of vicars in the west entrance porch and on the north wall towards the back there is a plaque placed there in 1863 by his surviving children and grandchildren.

- <https://huddersfieldparishchurch.org/>

Bradford

During the Industrial Revolution, Bradford boomed through the textile industry, especially in wool. For a time it could claim to be the wool capital of the world. As this industry declined in the mid-twentieth century, however, the city became less prosperous and has fallen behind its close neighbour and rival, Leeds. Like Huddersfield it is seeking to diversify, and in 2009 it became the first UNESCO City of Film in the world.

Although not specifically associated with Richard Oastler or Smith Wigglesworth, Bradford Cathedral is a good place to begin a pilgrimage visit to the city. It is set on a small hill above the modern shopping centre and provides an excellent setting for reflection and prayer close to the busyness of the city. Its cathedral status is relatively recent and it was originally a very old parish church which has been developed and enhanced in recent decades. It is somewhat crowded with memorials and additions for my taste, but you can still find a private space to focus your thoughts, if you wish.

Leaving the cathedral, head down the steps into the city centre and walk west (more or less) to Oastler's statue in Northgate Square. The statue forms the focus of a small and otherwise ordinary paved area outside the Oastler Shopping Centre. Interestingly, it is not just Oastler who is depicted but also two children he is helping. The simplicity of the inscription—his name and dates—suggests that his achievements were so well known at his death that there was no need to provide any details.

Places associated with Smith Wigglesworth are not pilgrimage sites in the conventional sense, but they do offer a telling contrast to more conventional monastic and church sites. They also take a bit of finding, whether by car or public transport! Going out from the city centre the nearest place to visit is the Bowland Street Mission Hall where Wigglesworth preached for over forty years. After years of neglect it has recently been purchased by an independent church called New Life Ministries, whose members are seeking to renovate it. Currently it is not open for public viewing, but seeing it tucked in amongst car repair workshops and Asian restaurants is a reminder of the realities of urban mission both today and a century ago.

A little further out is Lister Park where Wigglesworth preached in the open air. Cartwright Hall in the park is now a gallery and museum which give insight into the history and current life of Bradford. It is a short walk from the northern edge of the park to the home of Smith and Polly at number 70 Victor Road, a typical millstone grit terraced house in the shadow of Manningham textile works.

Prayer

God of all life,
we sometimes struggle to see you in the grit of our cities.
Thank you for those in previous generations
    who looked for you in these places.
As we wonder where to find you in our towns and cities
give us eyes to see you, ears to hear you,
    hearts to love you in the messiness,
and the desire to seek your justice for all people.

Practicalities

Huddersfield and Bradford

Huddersfield and Bradford both have good connections by road and rail. Huddersfield is just south of the M62, while Bradford is just north of it. For public transport across West Yorkshire see <https://www.wymetro.com/>.

Other places

Saltaire

About four miles north of Bradford is the planned town of Saltaire on the River Aire. It was opened in 1853 by the textile manufacturer and philanthropist Sir Titus Salt, as a way of improving the living conditions of his workers. Today the mill building contains creative businesses and gallery spaces. A deeply religious man, Salt also built a magnificent Congregational church in a classical style.

- <https://saltairevillage.info/>

Kirkstall Abbey

Following the River Aire downstream we come to the ruins of Kirkstall Abbey, north-west of Leeds city centre. This is another of Yorkshire's great Cistercian abbeys, founded here in 1152 by a group of monks from Fountains Abbey. It is in relatively good condition and offers another opportunity to learn more of the monastic life, as well as the subsequent use of the site.

- <https://museumsandgalleries.leeds.gov.uk/kirkstall-abbey/>

Leeds Minster

There has been a church on this site, in what is now the centre of Leeds, for over 1,200 years, and the church still preserves stone crosses carved before the year 1000. The vast expansion of Leeds resulted in the building of a new church, consecrated in 1841, which forms the current building. A short walk from Kirkgate to St Peter's Square leads to a blue plaque commemorating Richard Oastler, who was born here.

- <http://www.leedsminster.org/>

Dewsbury Minster

Dewsbury Minster is thought to have its origins in the preaching ministry of Paulinus (see Day 3) after which the Anglo-Saxons erected a stone cross and then a large church. In the 900s it was the mother church of a large area of the Pennines, and its important history led to its designation as a minster church in 1993, the first in England since the Reformation. The beautiful Paulinus Chapel is a peaceful space for prayer and reflection.

- <http://www.dewsburyminster.org.uk/>

Wakefield Cathedral
The cathedral traces its origins to an Anglo-Saxon church on this site over 1,000 years ago. It has since been much enlarged and altered. Today, in both worship and outlook, it is a place of welcome and support for all, with a special emphasis on the needy and disadvantaged.

- <https://www.wakefieldcathedral.org.uk/>

DAY 7

The West Riding, going south:
Recapping the themes

As we begin the last day of the pilgrimage, some of the main themes are reinforced by the people and places we encounter. We begin with the key builder of another of the great abbeys (Selby), move on to a pioneer of the spiritual life, and end in one of the great industrial cities, learning more about one approach to the Church's mission in the mid twentieth century. This variety of stories and engagement in the Christian life has been part of the journey throughout Yorkshire. It is both a rich source of inspiration and also a reminder of the challenge of telling a unified story of Christianity in this region. Christians and the Church have tried to make sense of their faith in many different contexts, and this southern part of God's Own County reflects that variety.

People

Hugh de Lacy (died around 1125)
The great buildings we have been visiting on this pilgrimage around Yorkshire were only built and maintained because many people over many years have worked hard for and loved these places. But we have also considered the significant individuals in the history of a place, and they deserve to be remembered. Selby Abbey is now one of the great parish churches of England, the first monastery to be founded in the North after the Norman Conquest and a rare example of an abbey church surviving the Reformation. While countless people have made this possible its

second abbot, Hugh de Lacy, played a key role in the building of the Abbey and in ensuring that it flourished.

Our knowledge of Hugh comes mainly from an anonymous monk of Selby who wrote a history of the Abbey about fifty years after Hugh's death. Hugh was born into a prominent Norman family; it is likely that he began his monastic life in Durham and saw the rebuilding of the great cathedral there. At some point he moved to Selby and the community saw his qualities and elected him as their prior, the assistant to the abbot. The anonymous history is perhaps a little starry-eyed when it says: "Those were the good old days when honesty flourished, goodness was much in evidence, valour and virtue reigned together." Nonetheless, Hugh stands out in the account of the abbots as hard-working, prayerful, concerned for the poor and an inspiring leader. His predecessor and at least two immediate successors were not well regarded, which suggests that the account was not just idealizing the past.

Selby Abbey had been founded in 1069 by direct order of King William, as a northern counterpart to his other great early abbey at Battle near Hastings. It was given extensive lands so that it could prosper under its first abbot, Benedict. He began well, but when two monks stole silver from the monastic treasury, he punished them mercilessly, finally castrating them. Unsurprisingly this led to massive rows in the community and beyond, to the extent that King William II ordered Benedict's arrest. Benedict resisted but soon came to realize his cause was hopeless and quietly retired.

This was the problematic background to Hugh's appointment as abbot, whose first task was to regain the trust of his fellow monks for the abbot's role within the community. He decided that the monastery's wooden buildings should be replaced with stone and so made good use of a quarry on abbey land at Fryston, contributing from his family's wealth to help meet the cost. More impressively he joined in the work by carrying stones and other material for the skilled workmen to use. Apparently he received the same weekly wage as the other workers but gave it away to the poor of the town. His energy and commitment ensured that much of the building was completed in his lifetime and can still be seen. The second pillar on the south side of the nave is known as Abbot Hugh's pillar, because it is decorated with a diamond pattern very similar to that seen in Durham Cathedral.

The anonymous history also emphasizes Hugh's charity and compassion. He felt deeply for others and showed this by giving away clothes and food. He was ready to serve the food for the brothers and made sure that food was made available to the poor. He also made regular visits to the sick.

After twenty-six years as abbot he wanted to retire and obtained permission from Archbishop Thurstan (see Day 5). When this became public, there was an outcry, but the archbishop supported him. The anonymous history thought that this was because Abbot Hugh had not wanted Thurstan as archbishop. Whatever the truth of the matter, Hugh made a farewell tour of many shrines in England, going south to St Albans and north to Durham. Two years later he died after a short illness and was buried with "great reverence".

Hugh is remembered for the way in which he combined personal devotion to God, care for the poor and needy and the ability to manage a complicated organization, undertaking a major building project. This practical piety was not shared by his successors, who seemed strong on devotion or practical management but not both. On our own pilgrimage here is a good moment to reflect on our own strengths and weaknesses. What and who might help us to use our strengths to God's glory and to overcome our weaknesses?

Richard Rolle (c.1300–49)

"He is mad," cried Rolle's sister when he cut up two of her dresses to make a hermit outfit. From this unconventional beginning there developed an inspiring and prolific writer on the spiritual life.

Some of God's people we have followed in our pilgrimage found their own calling in monastic communities. As we have just learned, this suited Hugh de Lacy very well, and we began our journey with Hilda and her community at Whitby (Day 1). But there were always a few people who struggled with that kind of life and set out on a more individual spiritual path, becoming hermits or anchorites. An early example was Robert Flower of Knaresborough (Day 5), and now we encounter Richard Rolle, the first English writer on the theme of mysticism. Rolle emphasized the centrality of responding to God's love rather than a purely intellectual approach to faith.

Our knowledge of him comes from a few hints in his many writings and from a collection of stories made after his death in the hope he might be canonized as a saint. He was born in a modest setting in Thornton-le-Dale, a few miles east of Pickering. He must have shown early promise, because the Archdeacon of Durham sponsored him to study at Oxford. However, he left without finishing his degree after several profound religious experiences. Returning home he asked his sister for two of her tunics, which he adapted together with his father's hood into a makeshift hermit's habit. Wearing this, he went to a nearby church, probably in Pickering, where he was found praying in the seat of the lady of the manor. He was taken in by her husband, John Dalton, and after Rolle preached a sermon which moved the congregation deeply Dalton recognized his potential and provided him with more suitable clothing and a place to stay.

Aged twenty-two, singing psalms in the Daltons' chapel, he had his first experience of God's love which he described as warmth, a sweet smell or taste, and the song of heaven. This became the centre of his spiritual experience, rather than the more conventional fasting, vigils and manual labour. He only attended Mass on feast days, when it was sung, preferring the "song of heaven". As he later wrote, "Jesus, I know no sweet delight than to sing my heart to you, the one that I love, the song of praise."

As a younger man he was critical of the usual approaches to religion, especially those in monasteries. He had his own difficulties; he lacked understanding and empathy for the religious life, and struggled in his relationships with women, even when he thought he was seeking their welfare. As he admits himself in his best-known book *The Fire of Love*, "Another [woman] rebuked me because I spoke of her great bosom as if it pleased me. She said, 'What business is it of yours whether it is big or little?' She was right." (Chapter 12) Following other rebukes from women with whom he seemed too familiar, he decided he must change, and as his character matured he was appreciated by both men and women for his spiritual advice.

For all the apparent simplicity of his vision of God's love and warmth he was very learned and wrote a significant collection of commentaries on the Bible and books on the spiritual life. He must have had access to libraries and the work of other scholars, and it is possible he spent time at the Sorbonne in Paris. He also lived near Northallerton for a time, but we do not know in any detail how he acquired his knowledge. He wrote in both Latin and English and was one of the first writers to use English for serious topics, a few decades before Geoffrey Chaucer. His books were widely distributed during and after his lifetime up to the Reformation. His translation of the Psalms into English for the anchorite Margaret Kirkby remained the only authorized English version for nearly 200 years.

Rolle's final move was to Hampole, where he became an adviser to the Cistercian nuns and to Margaret Kirkby. He died at Hampole on 30 September 1349, possibly as a result of the Black Death. He was buried there, and his tomb became a place of pilgrimage. Pilgrims reported the experiences of heavenly warmth, sweetness, and song that Rolle had described and even visions of the hermit. Around 1380 Margaret Kirkby moved to Hampole and with a few surviving nuns she collected stories of Rolle's life in the hope of his canonization. This never took place but his influence continued through the shrine and his writings.

His emphasis on personal experience of God's love undermined the authority of the official Church to some extent, particularly with regard to penance for sin. This was popular with ordinary people but less so with the clergy. There were genuine concerns that his experiential approach would lead to superstition and extremism, but his own moderation was also noted, and his writings were somewhat cautiously promoted by the Church. A good example of his moderation is found in these words from *The Fire of Love* on fasting:

> Yet the abstinence in which he lives should not be excessive, nor on the other hand should he display too much extravagance. Better for him slightly to exceed the limit if it is done in ignorance and with the sound intention of sustaining the body, than that he should, by the strict fasting and through physical weakness, be unable to sing. (Chapter 11)

In our own time Richard Rolle still provides a powerful and moving example of someone caught up in the love of God, someone warmed by the fire of the Holy Spirit and inspired to share that with others. Perhaps his sister was right in seeing him as mad when he began the hermit life, but over time he matured and was much valued for his spiritual fervour and wisdom. How do our own enthusiasms stay alive and mature?

Ted Wickham (1911–94)

The Church of England did not lose its appeal to working class people in the twentieth century; it was never there, according to the last character on this pilgrimage. A clergyman in Sheffield, Ted Wickham examined the Church's struggle to connect with working people and decided that it had never succeeded in doing so. He claimed that a new and different method was needed.

Ted Wickham was born in 1911 in Walthamstow, London, the fourth child in the family of three sons and three daughters of Edward Wickham, who worked for the Bank of England, and his wife Minnie Florence, who was of Huguenot descent. His mother's death when he was ten was a huge blow to Ted. He left school at fifteen, working as a clerk. Through his involvement in the Anglo-Catholic parish of St Philip, Tottenham, and his own intelligence and hard work, he completed a theology degree via evening classes. After further training he was ordained deacon in 1938 and priest in 1939 by the Bishop of Newcastle, and served as curate at Christ Church, Shieldfield, Newcastle upon Tyne. In 1941 he was appointed as chaplain to the large Royal Ordnance factory in Staffordshire, where he met Helen Moss, whom he married in 1944. They had three surviving children, though sadly three other children died in infancy.

In 1944 Wickham set up the Sheffield Industrial Mission (SIM) and became Sheffield diocesan missioner to industry, an experimental post he held until 1959. Bishop Leslie Hunter was aware of the gap between working people in the large industrial cities and the Church of England, except for rites of passage. The Labour and trade union movements believed that the Church was of no relevance or use to them. The work of Hunter and Wickham took a new approach to working people by first speaking to both trade unions and management in the labour-intensive heavy steel industry in Sheffield. Visits to factories and individuals only happened with the agreement of both sides of the industry. This approach was made easier because much of the work was done by comparatively small groups of men, who needed frequent breaks in the process of steel-making. Wickham was gifted at talking informally on the factory floor and in the canteens, speaking in a friendly and amusing cockney accent. Above all he could explain theology in understandable terms. His success led to the SIM becoming more permanent, and Wickham was made a residentiary canon of Sheffield Cathedral in 1950.

Unusually for an Anglican of his time he had excellent contacts with the Church in Europe, and was well known in the later 1940s among the leaders of the infant World Council of Churches. He related well both to the German Protestant Church—he could quote Luther and later theologians—and also to two French Roman Catholic radical movements, the Mission de France and the Mission de Paris. These were similar to the Sheffield Industrial Mission, which was expanded during the 1950s. By 1959 there were eight full-time chaplains visiting eighteen steel and engineering companies in Sheffield and Rotherham, and some departments of British Rail.

The growth of this team gave Wickham the opportunity to do detailed research from 1955 to 1957 into the history of the Church in Sheffield. This was when he concluded that the Church of England had not lost the working classes, but had never had them, even if Methodism had helped to develop the Labour movement. He felt that the nineteenth-century burst of church building in the cities had only led to the establishment of small, lower middle-class congregations. (Later research suggested that Sheffield was among the cities with the lowest rates of churchgoing and that Wickham's findings were incorrect elsewhere.) His book *Church and People in an Industrial City* (1957) was widely influential. His proposed solution was that the Church should first work with the trade unions and employers, and then with groups in their places of work.

Despite the book's influence, there was also opposition to Wickham's work. Parish clergy complained: "He didn't get people into the churches." His response was that the gap between most working people and most parish churches was too big to be crossed. Wickham could be abrasive, which makes his appointment as Bishop of Middleton, in Manchester, somewhat surprising. Apparently he said to friends, "I have been blackballed into the episcopacy." For the next twenty-three years he was effectively an assistant to the Bishop of Manchester, and was very restricted in following up the pioneering work he had begun in Sheffield. He continued to write but with much less impact than before. He was more fruitful in developing a night shelter for down-and-outs in Manchester, which grew into a network of houses for the homeless. He also worked with the new Salford University, becoming chairman of its council. He always enjoyed working with groups outside the established Church.

Ted Wickham died on 29 September 1994 in Salford, and as he was a keen mountaineer, his ashes were interred in the churchyard of the Climbers' Chapel, Wasdale Head, Cumbria. He was survived by his wife, son and two daughters. The Sheffield Industrial Mission and his book about Sheffield were his lasting achievements. Although the SIM went through difficult times, in the 1960s it re-emerged under a series of gifted leaders, becoming ecumenical and branching out into other workplaces as steel work declined in Sheffield. It was an inspiring forerunner of much workplace chaplaincy that continues to this day in Yorkshire and beyond.

Wickham's story is another reminder of the complex relationships between gifted leaders, the institution of the Church, groups in wider society and of individual people. Although a cathedral canon and then a bishop, he was often critical of his own church and in particular its failure to connect with working people. How far does any of this surprise you? How might his story with its ups and downs inform your own attempts to connect your faith with the rest of life?

Places

Selby

Selby has been a trading and market town for many centuries following its foundation by Abbot Benedict in 1069. Its position on the River Ouse, close to the Humber estuary, made it an important hub for trading, manufacturing and shipbuilding. The manufacturing and shipbuilding have ceased, and the town has struggled following the closure of the Selby coalfield. Civic pride is strong and is seeking to build on the heritage of the abbey. A fun feature is the use of the Three Swans logo derived from Benedict's vision: he was called to build a monastery in the place where he saw three swans swimming. Apparently there are now more than twenty-five examples of Three Swans around the town and the current Bishop of Selby features the Three Swans on his episcopal ring.

The abbey buildings of today were begun by Abbot Hugh over 900 years ago and were much more extensive until the Reformation. It acquired a very senior status as a "mitred" abbey, one of only two in the north of England. Its abbots then had the same status as a bishop. The building has been continuously developed and repaired. Among more recent developments was the addition of three bells to make twelve for the millennium and major restoration work around most of the building. These included new gargoyles, one of which represents John Sentamu, who retired as Archbishop of York in 2020. It can be found on the outside of the building on the south side towards the east end and is a distinctive image because it shows him wearing his glasses.

The church is open every day for visitors and it is well served with discreet descriptions of the building and its contents. There are free leaflets to guide you around the abbey, including "A Pilgrim's Guide" with brief details of significant features and suitable prayers to go with them. I am very impressed with the way the abbey community helps visitors and pilgrims to understand the building and how it can be used for prayer and reflection. There are a number of spaces offered for prayer so do take the opportunity.

- <https://www.selbyabbey.org.uk/>

Hampole and Adwick-le-Street

The tiny hamlet of Hampole has almost nothing to show of the convent that Rolle would have known and where he was buried, though excavations in 2018 revealed some foundations and there are a few humps and bumps in a field. The site is reached by following the path indicated by a new commemorative stone created by the York sculptor Charles Gurrey in 2018. The stone records a short phrase from Rolle, seeking to encapsulate his understanding of the spiritual life: "O good Jesu Thou has bound my heart in the thought of thy name and now I cannot but sing it."

The nearby town of Adwick-le-Street is an ancient settlement, on the line of the Roman road north, and hence a stopping off point for journeys over the centuries. St Laurence's Church is the parish church where Rolle himself would have worshipped. In recent years the building has been renovated to display its history more fully. The north, or Hampole, aisle includes information about Richard Rolle and there is a fine relief panel depicting Rolle made by Charles Gurrey in 2015. On my visit I noticed a fine stained-glass window commemorating St Francis of Assisi, another more famous saint who knew about the fire of God's love.

Do check the outside information board as a key may be required for access.

Sheffield

Personally I am very pleased to end this particular pilgrimage through Yorkshire at Sheffield Cathedral, for it is where I was ordained as a deacon and a priest in the 1980s. It has special and important memories for me. But I also believe Sheffield to be a good place to finish this journey because it stands for the massive change in Yorkshire and across the world from a rural past to an urban present and future. The challenges facing the cathedrals and churches in Sheffield are shared across the country and in many parts of the world.

Sheffield Cathedral was a large parish church for most of its history, becoming the cathedral of the new diocese in 1914. As the cathedral of one of the first steel cities in the world it is noticeable how many items within reflect the history of steel-making and also silversmithing. The main entrance to the cathedral is enhanced by a wonderful Lantern Tower, with abstract stained-glass dating from 1998, representing the Christian journey through life. If you turn round to face the entrance, on the right-hand side is a large painting of Christ over Sheffield from the 1950s by David Hepher. It divides opinion, but having first lived in Sheffield myself in the 1970s I find it a moving depiction of a city in transition after the Second World War, not least because Sheffield remains a city still discovering a future. As cathedrals go, it is relatively uncluttered, and I find the modern crypt a peaceful place for prayer and reflection. It might make for a good ending to this pilgrimage.

- <https://www.sheffieldcathedral.org/>

There is a recent short one-day pilgrimage route around Sheffield ending at the cathedral.

- <https://britishpilgrimage.org/portfolio/sheffield-cathedral-pilgrimage-in-a-day/>

While in the city centre you may also wish to visit the Roman Catholic cathedral of St Marie, since it is only a short walk down Fargate and left onto Norfolk Row. St Marie was built in the mid-nineteenth century for the expanding Roman Catholic population. It welcomes all visitors and has a very prayerful atmosphere. Nowadays it is a reminder of the growth of warm relationships between churches which in the past were hostile to one another.

- <https://stmariecathedral.org>

Prayer

Good Jesus,
Your holy name has been spoken in every part of this county
As this journey comes to its end
We pray for those who rejoice in that name
for those who have yet to know that name
for those who are troubled by that name
May we all share in the loving power of the name of Jesus
And so be made evermore truly into God's own people.

Practicalities

Selby
Selby is well served by trains and buses travelling in all directions, including Leeds, York, and Doncaster, and (by train) Hull. By car it can be reached along the A63 and A19, to link with other places on this pilgrimage.

Hampole and Adwick-le-Street

These places are easily reached by car off the A1, which still runs close to the old Great North Road. St Laurence's Church is five minutes' walk from the Adwick-le-Street station, which is on the line between Doncaster and Leeds. There is no public transport to Hampole.

Sheffield

Sheffield is easily reached by train, bus and car. Sheffield Cathedral is about ten minutes' walk from the train and bus stations.

Other places

Snaith Priory

Snaith Priory was a daughter church of Selby Abbey, and the present building is largely the work of the monks from Selby. It dates back to the twelfth century with additions completed in the thirteenth century. It was on the pilgrimage route between Canterbury and York and remains worth a visit when heading south from Selby, a journey of less than eight miles. At the time of writing it is being refurbished.

- <http://www.greatsnaith.org.uk/Snaith-History.html>

All Saints Darfield, Barnsley

About ten miles east of Adwick-le-Street is the lovely old church of All Saints Darfield. It is on one of the earliest Christian sites in South Yorkshire, and visitors are very welcome. Of special and poignant interest is the memorial in the churchyard to ten miners killed in an underground accident in 1886. Sadly these can be found in a number of churches, acknowledging the dangers of mining, and they are a significant reminder of the role of industry and the Church in this area over a long period.

- <http://www.darfieldallsaintschurch.org.uk/>

Barnsley

James Hudson Taylor was born in 1832, and was founder of the China Inland Mission, one of the largest Christian movements in the world. This organisation, which continues its work as OMF International, was responsible for taking over 800 missionaries to China. Taylor was brought up in Barnsley, the son of a pharmacist and lay preacher. Growing interest from Chinese Christians has led to the setting up of the Barnsley JHT trail with fourteen places of interest to visit.

- <http://www.jameshudsontaylor.org.uk/trail.html>

Roche Abbey

Roche Abbey was another Cistercian monastery, founded in 1147. Like Rievaulx and Fountains it is in a secluded and steep-sided valley. I remember taking our young children there to play on the grassy slopes and imbibe the atmosphere. It is well signed and maintained and easily visited on the way to Sheffield.

- <https://www.english-heritage.org.uk/visit/places/roche-abbey/>

A Personal Conclusion

I have been asked several times how long it has taken me to write this book, and the answer is "It all depends!" Most of the detailed research and writing has taken just over a year in between everything else I do. But I have been thinking about the possibility of this book for another ten years since I moved back to Yorkshire. And before that my thinking stretches back forty years to when I first lived in Sheffield and wanted to make sense of the place to which I had moved.

For me this has been a journey of reminders of places and people which have challenged and inspired me. Many of them have been part of family life: wet days in Whitby, watching sheep in the Dales, enjoying the buzz of the big cities are shared memories. I have been able to rediscover and appreciate the Yorkshire heritage of people, places and buildings and discover some new ones along the way. So here are just a few things that stand out for me as this particular pilgrimage journey comes to an end.

The connection between identity and place has been reinforced for me. Knowing more about individuals who have shaped these places deepens our own connections and shapes our identity. Long-standing and well-known examples of this are the stories of Hilda in Whitby and Wilberforce in Hull. I have noticed that in other places people value and appreciate those who have gone before. Among them are Robert Flower of Knaresborough, Richard Oastler across the West Riding and Richard Rolle in Hampole. Remembering them in their own places adds colour and identity to the people who live there now.

It is inevitable, when writing about people from the past, that many of them were of high status in their own day: someone had to write down their stories after all. I have been pleased and even a little surprised that it is also possible to connect with some more ordinary lives and to discover something of what their faith meant to them. Besides meeting bishops, entrepreneurs and even a king, I have also learned more about my faith through a keeper of animals, a housewife and a plumber. What stands out for me in all these stories is the dedication and integrity of these people. It is not that they were perfect, but they had a deep commitment to pursue God's way through Jesus Christ. Even though I have not been called to live exactly the same lives as they, their struggles and dedication continue to challenge and inspire me.

Finally, it is particularly noticeable that the idea of pilgrimage continues to resonate with many people. When I first moved to Yorkshire, I suspect that pilgrimage for most people was either an unknown idea or associated with medieval Catholicism and dusty relics. Since then there has been a growth in travel generally and part of that is a wider appreciation of learning more about ourselves as well as the world around us by encountering new people in new places. Pilgrimage is now seen to take many forms across many religions and even non-religious activities. It is about making a journey with a purpose and an openness to personal growth and development. This particular journey with God's Own People across God's Own County has deepened my appreciation of the Christian heritage of Yorkshire. The present county would be very different without that heritage, even though that is not always obvious today.

My hope and prayer is that the journeys you undertake with the help of this book will deepen your own appreciation of that heritage and, beyond that, your own encounter with the living God in Jesus Christ.

Some further reading

Hilda
Bede, *Ecclesiastical History* Book 4, chapters 23 and 24.

Cedd and Chad
Bede, *Ecclesiastical History* Book 3, chapters 21, 22, 23, 28; Book 4, chapter 3.

Aelred of Rievaulx
Paul Diemer, *Aelred of Rievaulx* (Leominster: Gracewing, 1997).

John of Beverley
Bede, *Ecclesiastical History* Book 5, chapters 2 to 6.

William Wilberforce
William Hague, *William Wilberforce: The Life of the Great Anti-Slave Trade Campaigner* (London: HarperPress, 2007).
A sympathetic portrait by another Yorkshireman and an experienced modern politician.

Robert Aske
Geoffrey Moorhouse, *The Pilgrimage of Grace: The rebellion that shook Henry VIII's throne* (London: Weidenfeld and Nicolson, 2002).
A very readable history of the Pilgrimage of Grace and Robert Aske's role as its emerging leader.

Edwin and Paulinus
Bede, *Ecclesiastical History* Book 2, chapters 9 to 17, 20.

Alcuin of York
Douglas Dales, *Alcuin: His Life and Legacy* (Cambridge: James Clarke & Co, 2012).

John Thornton
Sarah Brown, *Apocalypse: The Great East Window of York Minster* (Third Millennium Publishing, 2014).
<https://yorkminster.org/discover/behind-the-scenes/restoring-an-international-work-of-art/>

David Watson
David Watson, *You Are My God* (London: Hodder, 1983).
This is Watson's autobiography. I have also found Matthew Porter's Grove booklet very helpful, and there are two longer biographies available, including Saunders and Sansom.

Margaret Clitherow
Peter Lake and Michael Questier, *The Trials of Margaret Clitherow: Persecution, Martyrdom and the Politics of Sanctity in Elizabethan England* (London: Continuum, 2011).

Mary Ward
Gillian Orchard (ed.), *Till God Wills* (London: DLT, 1985).
A collection of some of Mary Ward's writings, together with a short biography.

Joseph Rowntree
His inspiring and insightful Founder's Memorandum, setting out principles for his charities: <https://www.jrf.org.uk/about-us/our-heritage/lasting-vision-change>.

Wilfrid
Bede, *Ecclesiastical History* Book 3, chapter 25, 28; Book 4, chapter 2, 13, 16, 19; Book 5, chapter 19.
Eddius Stephanus, 'Life of Wilfrid' in *The Age of Bede* (Harmondsworth: Penguin, 1983).

Robert of Knaresborough
Frank Bottomley, *St Robert of Knaresborough* (1993).

Thurstan
Donald Nicholl, *Thurstan: Archbishop of York, 1114–1140* (York: Stonegate Press, 1964).
This book might be obtainable from a library, otherwise it is a case of piecing together information from the internet and other sources.

Henry Venn
Stephen Tomkins, *The Clapham Sect* (Oxford: Lion Hudson, 2010).
See especially chapter 2 for a brief biography of Henry Venn and his impact on other evangelical leaders.

Richard Oastler
There are no recent books on Oastler. This newspaper clipping from 2018 gives a very brief summary: <https://yorkshirereporter.co.uk/richard-oastler-factory-king/>.

Smith Wigglesworth
Philip Taylor, *In the Steps of Smith Wigglesworth: Exploring Key Locations in the Life of the Legendary Healing Evangelist* (2007).

Hugh de Lacy
A short mention in Selby Abbey guidebook (2013) available at the abbey.
He is also mentioned in Janet Burton, *Monastic and Religious Orders in Britain 1000–1300* (Cambridge: Cambridge University Press, 1994). This book provides a very good overview of the monastic movement.

Richard Rolle
The Fire of Love, trans. Clifton Wolters (Harmondsworth: Penguin, 1972).
His most well-known work and includes a short biography.

Ted Wickham

<http://www.calmview.eu/SheffieldArchives/CalmView/Record.
    aspx?src=CalmView.Catalog&id=DIOC%2FIM>
Mainly a history of Sheffield Industrial Mission with some references
    to Wickham.
John Rogerson (ed.), *Industrial Mission in a Changing World* (Sheffield:
    Sheffield Academic Press, 1996).
Academic papers on the work of Sheffield Industrial Mission,
    including the role of Wickham.

Detailed information on twelve of the churches mentioned here can be
found in Simon Jenkins, *England's Thousand Best Churches* (London:
Penguin, 2002).

In order of appearance in this book they are: Whitby St Mary,
Lastingham St Mary, Beverley Minster, Beverley St Mary, Hull Minster,
Bridlington Priory, Patrington St Patrick, Howden Minster, York St
Michael-le-Belfrey, Studley Royal St Mary, Knaresborough St John and
Selby Abbey.

Lightning Source UK Ltd.
Milton Keynes UK
UKHW021438210720
366908UK00006B/272